♦ GRANNY'S DRAWERS ♦

*Four Generations
of Family Favorites*

Karen Harris

Carolina Publishing
Chapel Hill, North Carolina

Cover illustration by Marlene Loznicka
Morehead City, North Carolina

ISBN: 1-886690-50-2
First Printing, 5,000, October, 1995
Second Printing, 5,000, August, 1996
Third Printing, 15,000, January, 1997
Fourth Printing, 7,500, September, 1997
Fifth Printing, 3,000, May, 1999
Sixth Printing, 7,500, June 1999

Carolina Publishing Company
Post Office Box 972
Apex, North Carolina 27502
Email: carolinapublish@mindspring.com
Phone: 800-256-9908

Printed in the USA by

WIMMER

The Wimmer Companies

Memphis

1-800-548-2537

◆ DEDICATION ◆

Gladys Biggers Allen

*This book is dedicated to our grandmother,
who showed us that a life of loving and giving
will be richly rewarded.*

You may go back to your special diets, friends. I get more nourishment out of musty memories than the modern sucker gets from a well-rounded fare that is guaranteed to keep him both thin and unhappy with the cook.

Robert C. Ruark

♦ INTRODUCTION ♦

Granny's Drawers is a labor of love. I began this journey when I realized that no one in our family had Granny's recipe for fried chicken, which was the *best* fried chicken I've ever tasted. While watching Granny battle Alzheimers, I realized that it was important for us to accumulate our family recipes now, before many of our favorite dishes and memories were lost or forgotten. With the help of my family, we accomplished our goal. The only missing recipe is Granny's fried chicken, which she has taken with her to a higher place.

The little girl on the cover is me. I was the granddaughter who stayed with Granny on Saturday nights, went with her to Park Road Baptist Church on Sundays and ate her fried chicken for Sunday lunch. Often, I would rummage through Granny's drawers to look at old photos and wonder who all those funny looking people were. To my surprise, I discovered that many of them were close relatives.

Christmas 1994 was a special day for our family. To celebrate Granny's life and remember her passing, I unveiled the first draft of *Granny's Drawers*. What joy and happy pandemonium! Since my mother was one of the few at the gathering who didn't need reading glasses, she could actually read the cookbook that evening. She sat on a sofa with Uncle Parks, and read the picture captions to him. At one point, she looked up and found tears rolling down his cheeks. As Uncle Bob was leaving, he said "in all of the years I knew Mrs. Allen (Granny), I never saw her cry; I'm certain if she were here tonight, she'd be crying." I told him that it would be alright, so long as her tears were happy ones. At that point, I had to walk away before he made *me* cry...

Karen Harris

♦ ACKNOWLEDGMENTS ♦

Without a supportive and patient family, *Granny's Drawers* would not have been possible. I owe a special thanks to my mother, Margaret Young, who taught me many lessons about love, commitment, and courage. This book is a reflection of the many gifts she has given me. My thanks to *the* aunts, Gwen Allen, Pat Rush, Jackie Brown, and Eleanor Helms. Their love and good cooking have nourished our family for years. Thanks are also due my sister-in-law and my cousins, who contributed many of the "modern" recipes to this collection; Betty Young, Kathy Eudy, Janet Allen, Trisha Weeks, Debbie Brown, Libby Brown, Sharon Mack, and Deborah Alston. Many other family members contributed to this effort, including Martha Helms, Kathryn Alston, Louise Rush, Ida Helms, Cynthia and Ruth Biggers, Paul Allen, and Bob Rush. Charlie Young, my father, contributed no recipes–only a sense of joy and wonderment with *learning* that has served me all of my life.

Many special friends helped with the production of *Granny's Drawers*. My thanks to Marlene Loznicka, who painted the cover illustration of me plundering through Granny's drawers. Fred Zaytoun, owner of Design Press, provided me invaluable guidance on book design and printing options. Laura Williams edited and proofed the recipes, while Charlotte Ranz and Jess McLamb provided me a critical review of design and layout.

These comments are not complete without a *special* thanks to my husband, Sam, who encouraged me to tackle this project. His words of encouragement and love for this project made *Granny's Drawers* possible.

♦ CONTENTS ♦

◆ APPETIZERS ◆
AND BEVERAGES

Cynthia Biggers

*Cynthia, Granny's sister, regrets to this
day selling her 1928 Model-T
to her boyfriend for $75.*

My family's love for food dates back four generations to Granny's family, the Biggers. Granny was raised, along with four sisters and four brothers, on a large farm in Clover, South Carolina, where cotton was the cash crop and vegetables were raised to feed the family. In 1923, Granny's brother, Howard, began delivering produce to Charlotte with one truck. Brothers Bill, George and Oren later joined Howard at the business, Biggers Brothers, which grew over time to became one of the largest produce wholesalers in the southeast.

Three of Granny's sisters (Cynthia, Ruth, and Eula) were school teachers in Clover. They were among those southern teachers who taught children to read and think and to have good manners. Cynthia and Ruth now live next door to the old home place; they benevolently smile at the questions of grand-nieces, who wonder at their dignity, grace and wisdom.

Granny and her sister Margaret went into bookkeeping, the other field open to "genteel" young ladies during the 1920's. Granny moved to Charlotte, where she was hired by Paul Allen to be the bookkeeper for his company. According to family lore, she was engaged to another young man when she went to work for my (future) grandfather. He successfully "wooed" her away, and they married in 1927.

◆ PINEAPPLE ◆
CHEESE BALL

2	8-ounce packages cream cheese, softened
1	8 1/4-ounce can crushed drained pineapple
1	green pepper, minced
1	onion, minced
1	tablespoon seasoned salt
1	cup chopped pecans
1	fresh pineapple
	Crackers

Combine the cream cheese, pineapple, green pepper, onion, and salt until well blended. Add pecans and mix well. Prepare 24 hours in advance and refrigerate.

To serve: Cut the pineapple in half lengthwise and hollow out. Mound cheese mixture in each pineapple half and sprinkle pecans on top. Serve with crackers.

Yields: 3 cups

Jackie Brown

◆ BUDDIG BEEF ◆ CHEESE BALL

2	8-ounce packages cream cheese
1	4-ounce package cream cheese
3	packages Buddig Beef, chopped
2	teaspoons Worcestershire sauce
2	teaspoons Accent
1	small onion, chopped
	Crackers

Mix the cream cheese with two packages of Buddig Beef. Add the Worcestershire sauce, Accent and onion and mix well. Roll the cheese ball in the remaining package of Buddig Beef. Refrigerate. Serve with crackers.

Yields: 3 cups

Kathy Eudy

◆ GOUDA CHEESE ◆
APPETIZER

1   *small package Gouda cheese*
     Dijon mustard
1   *small can Crescent Rolls (4 roll package)*
     Triscuit Crackers

Preheat oven to 350 degrees. Remove wrapper and soften the cheese in the microwave. Cover the cheese with mustard. Wrap the cheese in the bread dough and pinch the sides of the dough closed.

Place on cookie sheet and bake at 350 degrees for 15 to 20 minutes. Serve with crackers.

Yields: cheese weight will determine number of servings

Sharon Mack

◆ CHEESE CRACKERS ◆

Easy to make and can be prepared well in advance.

1/2	pound New York sharp cheese, grated
3/4	stick margarine
1	cup all-purpose flour
1/4	teaspoon salt
	Dash of red pepper
1	cup whole pecans

Combine the cheese, margarine, flour, salt and pepper. Shape into 2 rolls and refrigerate.

Preheat oven to 350 degrees. Slice cheese thin, place on cookie sheet and place pecans on top. Bake at 350 degrees until done, approximately 9 minutes.

Yields: 36 crackers

Eleanor Helms

◆ SPINACH DIP ◆

1	10-ounce package frozen spinach, thawed and drained
1	cup sour cream
3/4	cup mayonnaise
1	cup water chestnuts
1	package Knorr vegetable soup mix
	Pepperidge Farm Butterfly Crackers

Mix the spinach, sour cream, mayonnaise, chestnuts, and soup mix. Serve with crackers.

Yields: 2 cups

Eleanor Helms

◆ ARTICHOKE DIP ◆

2	cans artichoke hearts
1	cup grated Parmesan cheese
1	cup mayonnaise
	Crackers or raw vegetables

Preheat oven to 350 degrees. Drain and rinse artichoke hearts. Chop artichoke hearts into small pieces. Mix in cheese and mayonnaise. Spread into shallow pyrex dish. Bake at 350 degrees for 20 minutes. Serve with crackers.

Variation: Add a dash of lemon juice.

Yields: 3 cups

Sharon Mack
Deborah Alston

◆ HOT ARTICHOKE DIP ◆

1	*14-ounce can artichokes, drained and chopped*
1	*clove garlic, mashed, or 4 drops garlic juice*
1	*cup mayonnaise*
1/2	*teaspoon Worcestershire sauce, optional*
1	*cup grated Parmesan cheese*
	Freshly ground pepper to taste
	Paprika or minced parsley to taste
	Crackers or taco chips

Preheat oven to 350 degrees. Combine the artichokes, garlic, mayonnaise, Worcestershire sauce, Parmesan cheese, pepper and paprika in small greased baking dish. Bake at 350 degrees for 20 to 25 minutes. Serve hot with crackers or taco chips.

Variation: Add a 4-ounce can of chopped green chilies, seeded.

Yields: 2 cups

Eleanor Helms

♦ TUNA DIP ♦

1 8-ounce package cream cheese, softened
2 tablespoons crumbled blue cheese
1 6 1/2-ounce can tuna, drained
1/2 cup sour cream
2 teaspoons dried minced onions
1 3 or 4-ounce jar pimentos, drained
1 tablespoon lemon juice
1 tablespoon water
 Crackers

Place the cream cheese, blue cheese, tuna, sour cream, onions, pimento, lemon juice and water in an electric blender. Blend at high speed until mixture is thoroughly blended, about 30 seconds. Chill several hours. Serve with crackers.

Yields: 2 cups

Margaret Young

♦ ONION DIP ♦

1 16-ounce jar mayonnaise
1 16-ounce package sour cream
3 tablespoons minced onions
1 teaspoon parsley flakes
1 teaspoon Lowery's seasoned salt
 Potato chips or fresh vegetables

Combine all ingredients and mix well. Serve with chips or fresh vegetables.

Yields: 2 cups

Janet Allen

♦ SHRIMP DIP ♦

1	pound popcorn shrimp, boiled and chopped
1	small bottle ketchup
1/2	large package cream cheese, softened
	Dash Worcestershire sauce
	Crackers

Combine the shrimp, ketchup, cream cheese and Worcestershire sauce and chill. Serve with crackers.

Yields: 6 cups

Eleanor Helms

♦HOT CRAB MEAT DIP♦

1	8-ounce package cream cheese, softened
2	tablespoons milk, warm
1	6 1/2-ounce can king crab meat, rinsed
2	tablespoons chopped onion
1/2	teaspoon creamy style horseradish
1/4	teaspoon salt
	Dash of pepper
1/3	cup sliced almonds
	Crackers

Preheat oven to 375 degrees. Mix the cream cheese, milk, crab meat, onion, horseradish, salt and pepper. Put in baking dish and top with almonds. Bake at 375 degrees for 15 minutes. Serve with crackers.

Yields: 2 cups

Margaret Young

♦ CRABBIES ♦

1/2	cup margarine or butter, softened
1 1/2	tablespoons mayonnaise
1/2	teaspoon garlic salt
1/2	teaspoon seasoned salt
1	small jar sharp pasteurized cheese
1	6 1/2-ounce can crab meat, drained
6	English muffins, split

Preheat oven on Broil. Mix the margarine, mayonnaise, garlic salt, seasoned salt, cheese, and crab meat. Spread on muffin halves. Broil until bubbly hot. Cut each muffin half into 6 pie-shaped pieces.

Yields: 10 servings

Deborah Alston

◆ VEGETABLE ◆
SANDWICHES

1/4   cup chopped celery
1/4   cup chopped onions
1/4   cup chopped green pepper
1/4   cup sliced cucumber
3/4   cup carrots (2-3 carrots)
1   8-ounce package cream cheese, softened
2   tablespoons mayonnaise
      Salt and pepper to taste
      Bread or crackers

In an electric blender, chop the celery, onions, green pepper, cucumber and carrots. Add the cream cheese and mayonnaise to the vegetable mixture. Add salt and pepper to taste. Serve on bread or crackers.

Yields: 2 cups

Margaret Young

◆ HAM AND ◆
POPPY SEED ROLLS

1/2	pound margarine or butter, softened
3	tablespoons prepared mustard
3	tablespoons poppy seeds
1	teaspoon Worcestershire sauce
1	medium onion, finely diced
1/2	pound thinly-sliced boiled ham
1/2	pound thinly-sliced Swiss cheese
3	packages Pepperidge Farm Party Rolls

Preheat oven to 400 degrees. Combine margarine, mustard, poppy seeds, Worcestershire sauce, and onion. Slice all rolls, leaving them attached. Spread both sides of the rolls with the margarine mixture. Place 1 layer of ham and 1 layer of cheese between the rolls, cutting ham and cheese to fit as necessary.

Place on cookie sheet and bake at 400 degrees for 10 to 15 minutes. Rolls may be prepared in advance and refrigerated or frozen for short period of time before baking.

Yields: 60 rolls

Jackie Brown

◆FRENCH BREAD PIZZA◆

Pizza crust:
> Large loaf French bread, split lengthwise
> Butter, softened

Pizza sauce:

1	6-ounce can tomato paste
1	8-ounce can tomato sauce
1/2	teaspoon garlic powder
1/2	teaspoon sweet basil leaves, crumbled
1/2	teaspoon oregano leaves, crumbled
1	teaspoon dried parsley flakes
1/4	cup Parmesan cheese

Pizza topping:

12	ounces mozzarella cheese, grated and divided
1	cup cooked ground beef or pork sausage
	Pepperoni slices
1/2	cup chopped green pepper
1	cup sliced fresh mushrooms

Set oven on broil. Lightly butter the cut sides of the bread and place on cookie sheet. Toast bread until light brown, watching bread carefully.

Reduce oven to 450 degrees. Combine all of the sauce ingredients in a small saucepan. Simmer the sauce on low heat for five minutes. Spread sauce on the cut sides of bread and sprinkle 8 ounces of cheese on sauce. Spread meat and vegetables evenly over the cheese. Sprinkle on the remaining 4 ounces of cheese. Bake at 450 degrees for 10 to 12 minutes until cheese melts.

Yields: 4 to 6 servings

Bob Rush

◆ SAUSAGE BALLS ◆

1	10-ounce package sharp cheese
1	pound hot sausage
2	cups Bisquick

Grate the cheese and mix well with the sausage and Bisquick. Roll mixture into balls 1 1/2-inches in diameter. Refrigerate until ready to cook.

Preheat oven to 400 degrees. Place in pan with sides to prevent sausage fat from draining into the stove. Bake at 400 degrees for approximately 20 minutes.

Yields: 48 sausage balls

Eleanor Helms

◆ HERB MINT TEA ◆

6	Earl Grey tea bags
2	quarts water, boiling hot
	Juice of 6 lemons, squeezed
1 1/2	cups sugar
	Handful spearmint leaves

Steep tea in hot water. Heat lemon juice and sugar to dissolve. Steep the mint leaves in 1 cup hot water, covered, for 10 to 12 minutes. Remove mint and add water to brewed tea.

Yields: 2 quarts

Eleanor Helms

◆INSTANT RUSSIAN TEA◆

One of Granny's favorites! She always kept a jar of tea mix in the kitchen during the winter months for a quick cup of spicy, hot tea.

2	cups Tang
1/2 to 3/4	cup instant tea
1	teaspoon cinnamon
1	cup sugar
1/2	teaspoon cloves

Combine the Tang, tea, cinnamon, sugar and cloves and blend well. Store in an airtight container. To serve, pour boiling water over 2 teaspoons of the tea mixture in a cup.

Yields: 4 cups mix

Jackie Brown

◆ PINEAPPLE PUNCH ◆

2	packages orange or lemon Kool-Ade
2	cups sugar
1	large can crushed pineapple
1	large can frozen orange juice
1	gallon water

Combine the Kool-Ade, sugar, pineapple and orange juice and mix well. Add enough water to make 1 gallon. Serve with ice.

Yields: 1 gallon

Margaret Young

◆ HOT SPICED ◆
PERCOLATOR PUNCH

1 3/4	cups water
2 1/4	cups pineapple juice
2	cups cranberry juice
1	tablespoon whole cloves
1/2	tablespoon allspice
3	sticks cinnamon, broken
1/4	teaspoon salt
1/2	cup light brown sugar

Put the water, pineapple and cranberry juices in the bottom of an 8-cup percolator. Place the cloves, allspice, cinnamon, salt and sugar in the percolator basket. Perk for 10 minutes or until spices permeate. Serve hot.

Yields: 8 to 10 servings

Eleanor Helms

✦ CHRISTMAS CIDER ✦

1/2   gallon cider
1 1/2   quarts cranberry juice
4 to 6   cloves
2-3   sticks cinnamon
1/4   cup brown sugar

Combine the cider, cranberry juice, cloves, cinnamon and sugar in a large saucepan. Bring to a boil over medium heat, stirring frequently. Cover and reduce heat. Simmer 10 minutes. Serve warm.

Yields: approximately 1 gallon

Eleanor Helms

◆ SOUPS AND EGGS ◆

Paul and Margaret Allen

In 1932, riding goat carts was a "big thing" on 36th Street in Charlotte, North Carolina.

Paul and Margaret are the eldest of Granny's five children. Paul, the only son, has been as "in-charge" in later life, as he was in the goat cart in 1932. In fact, Paul led Margaret to be a tomboy, playing football and climbing trees with the boys. After being told by her father not to play football, Margaret broke her arm in a scrimmage game. She hid her injury from her parents by paying sister Pat to do her chores. Months later, Margaret's injury was discovered when she went to the doctor with poison ivy. That ended her days of football glory.

Margaret developed an early love for cooking, and Paul loved the results. Paul's favorite was a German Chocolate Cake (page 214). While serving in the military in Korea, he begged Margaret to send him his favorite cake. The Red Cross, however, said that cakes were not on the Army's approved list for mailing overseas. Paul persisted with requests, until Margaret relented and sent him one.

Paul received the cake at an evening mail call and took it back to his tent, where he and his buddies ate it in the dark. One of the fellas commented, "This is the best cheesecake I've ever tasted." Since Paul knew Margaret wouldn't be sending him a cheesecake, he quietly stopped eating it. (The next morning, Paul discovered that the cake was green with mold). Paul never requested another cake during his tour of duty in Korea.

♦ GENOA-STYLE ♦ MINESTRONE

2	cups chopped onions
1	cup sliced celery
1/4	cup chopped fresh parsley
2	cloves garlic, minced
1/4	cup olive oil
5	cups beef broth
3 1/2	cups water
1/2	cup dry red wine (or water)
1	16-ounce can tomatoes, cut-up
1	15-ounce can tomato sauce
1	15-ounce can kidney beans (not drained)
1	16-ounce can garbonzo beans (not drained)
2	cups coarsely chopped cabbage
1	cup sliced carrots
2	teaspoons dry basil
1/2	teaspoon salt
1/4	teaspoon pepper
1	teaspoon sugar
1 1/2	cups sliced zucchini
1	cup frozen cut green beans
1	cup broken spaghetti or elbow macaroni
	Parmesan cheese

In an 8-quart pan, saute the onions, celery, parsley and garlic in the oil until the onions are transparent. Stir in the broth, water, wine, tomatoes, tomato sauce, cabbage, carrots, basil, salt, and pepper. Bring to a boil, reduce heat and simmer for 1 hour. Stir in the sugar, zucchini, green beans, and noodles. Simmer an additional 15 to 20 minutes. Sprinkle with Parmesan cheese and serve.

Yields: 10 to 12 servings

Martha Helms

◆FRENCH ONION SOUP◆

2	tablespoons margarine or butter
	Vegetable cooking spray
6	large onions, thinly sliced (3 pounds)
2	10 1/2-ounce cans beef consomme, undiluted
1	13 3/4-ounce can ready-to-serve, no-salt-added, fat-free beef flavored broth
1 1/3	cups water
1/4	cup Chablis or other dry white wine
1/4	teaspoon freshly ground pepper
6	1-inch thick slices French bread
1/4	cup grated Parmesan cheese

Melt the margarine in a Dutch oven coated with cooking spray. Add the onions and stir often; saute over medium heat for 5 minutes. Add one can of beef consomme. Cook over low heat 30 minutes. Gradually add remaining beef consomme, beef broth, water, wine and pepper. Bring to a boil and simmer and 10 minutes.

Place bread slices on a baking sheet and sprinkle with Parmesan cheese. Broil until golden brown. Ladle soup into bowls and top with a slice of toasted bread.

Yields: 7 servings

Pat Rush

◆ COMPANY ◆
ONION SOUP

4 *tablespoons margarine*
4 *large Vidalia or Walla Walla onions, sliced*
1 *tablespoon sugar*
6 *cups beef broth, divided*
2 *tablespoons Worcestershire sauce*
 Salt and pepper to taste
4 *thick slices French bread*
 Additional margarine
1 *clove garlic, halved, or garlic salt*
1 *cup (4-ounces) shredded Gruyere or Swiss cheese*

In a Dutch oven, melt the margarine over medium heat. Saute onions until tender. Sprinkle sugar over onions. Reduce heat and cook about 20 minutes, stirring occasionally until onions are caramelized. Add three cups of the broth and simmer for 15 minutes. Add the remaining broth, Worcestershire sauce, salt and pepper. Cover and simmer for 30 to 40 minutes.

While the soup is cooking, spread both sides of bread with additional margarine; sprinkle with garlic salt or rub with the cut side of a garlic clove. Broil the bread until golden brown, then turn and brown other side. Ladle soup into individual ovenproof soup bowls. Float a slice of the bread in each bowl and sprinkle with cheese. Broil until cheese is melted and bubbly. Serve immediately.

Yields: 4 servings

Pat Rush

◆ CORN CHOWDER ◆

2	tablespoons margarine
1/2	cup chopped onions
1/2	cup chopped celery
1	tablespoon all-purpose flour
4	cups skim milk
1	17-ounce can cream-style corn
1/4	teaspoon salt
1/4	teaspoon white pepper
1/4	teaspoon dried thyme
1/8	teaspoon paprika

Melt the margarine in a Dutch oven; saute the onions and celery until tender. Add the flour and cook one minute. Gradually add the milk and stir until the soup reaches a boil. Stir in the corn, salt, pepper and paprika. Reduce the heat and simmer for 20 minutes. Stir occasionally.

Yields: 6 servings

Karen Harris

◆ CHICKEN ◆
CORN CHOWDER

Easy to make and delicious!

1/2	cup finely chopped onion
1/2	cup water
2	5-ounce cans cooked chicken
2	17-ounce cans creamed corn
3	cups milk
	Salt and pepper to taste
1 1/2	cups (6-ounces) grated Cheddar cheese

Add onion and water to large heavy saucepan. Cook until onion is tender. Pour off water. Add chicken, corn, milk, salt and pepper. Bring to a boil. Reduce heat. Gradually add the cheese, stirring until the cheese is melted.

Yields: 6 servings

Karen Harris

♦ CALIFORNIA ♦
CHEESE SOUP

1	quart water
2	chicken bouillon cubes
1	cup chopped celery
1/2	cup diced onion
2 1/2	cups diced, peeled potatoes
1	cup diced carrots
1	16-ounce package California Blend vegetables
2	10 3/4-ounce cans condensed cream of chicken soup
1	pound processed cheese, cubed

In a Dutch oven, bring the water to a boil. Add the bouillon cubes, celery, onion, potatoes, carrots and mixed vegetables. Reduce heat, cover, and simmer for approximately 30 minutes, until all vegetables are tender. Stir in the chicken soup and cheese. Cook until soup is heated through and the cheese is melted.

Yields: 10 to 12 servings

Pat Rush

♦ CHEESE ♦
BROCCOLI SOUP

2	tablespoons corn oil
1	medium onion, chopped
6	cups water
6	chicken bouillon cubes
1	8-ounce package fine egg noodles
1	teaspoon salt
2	10-ounce packages frozen chopped broccoli
1/8	teaspoon garlic powder
6	cups milk
1	pound Velveeta cheese, cubed
	Salt and pepper to taste

Saute the onion in oil over medium-high heat for three minutes. Add the water and bouillon cubes and heat to boiling. Gradually add the noodles so mixture continues to boil. Cook for three minutes. Add the broccoli and garlic powder. Return to a boil and cook for four minutes. Add the milk, cheese, salt and pepper to taste. Heat through to melt the cheese. This soup can be frozen.

Yields: 12 servings

Martha Helms

◆ CREAM OF ◆
BROCCOLI SOUP

1	bunch fresh broccoli (about 1 1/2 cups)
1	medium onion, chopped (about 1/2 cup)
2	tablespoons margarine or butter
1	Idaho potato, diced (1 cup)
2	13 3/4-ounce cans chicken broth
1	teaspoon salt
1/4	teaspoon pepper
1	cup light cream
1/8	teaspoon nutmeg

Trim broccoli, steam for 5 to 8 minutes and drain. Saute the onion in the margarine for 5 minutes or until transparent. Add potatoes, chicken broth, salt and pepper. Bring to a boil then reduce heat and simmer for 15 minutes.

Add broccoli to soup and simmer for 5 minutes. Put soup in blender and puree. Return to pan; add the cream and nutmeg. Heat through and serve.

Yields: 6 servings

Margaret Young

◆ WISCONSIN ◆
POTATO CHEESE SOUP

2	tablespoons margarine
1/3	cup chopped celery
1/3	cup chopped onion
4	cups diced peeled potatoes
3	cups chicken broth
2	cups milk
1 1/2	teaspoons salt
1/4	teaspoon pepper
	Dash paprika
2	cups (8-ounces) grated cheddar cheese
	Croutons
	Parsley for garnish

In a large saucepan, melt the margarine over medium-high heat. Saute the celery and onion until tender. Add the potatoes and broth. Cover and simmer until the potatoes are tender, about 12 minutes. Stir in the milk, salt, pepper, and paprika. Add the cheese and heat only until melted. Garnish with croutons and parsley.

Yields: 8 servings

Pat Rush

♦ CHICKEN ♦
NOODLE SOUP

4	chicken breasts
	Celery salt
	Onion Salt
8	cups water
1	cup noodles, cooked
1/4	teaspoon thyme
1/2	bay leaf
2	carrots, coarsely grated
3/4	cup chopped celery (2 stalks)
6	peppercorns
1	tablespoon salt
1	onion, chopped

Season the chicken with celery salt and onion salt. Boil the chicken for about one hour in water. Remove the chicken from the pot and cut into bite-size pieces. Add the noodles, thyme and bay leaf to the chicken broth. Cook the broth for 10 minutes. Add the chicken, carrots, celery, peppercorns, salt and onion to the chicken broth. Simmer for 45 minutes to one hour.

Yields: 8 servings

Eleanor Helms

♦ CHICKEN ♦
GUMBO SOUP

4	skinless chicken breasts
2	large packages frozen okra
2	carrots
1	medium onion
2	stalks celery
1	can green peas
1	17-ounce can creamed corn
1	46-ounce can V-8 juice
1	gallon water (as needed)
1/4	cup sugar
1	tablespoon salt
1	teaspoon pepper
1	teaspoon celery seed
1	chicken bouillon cube

Boil the chicken for one hour, or until done. Remove the chicken from bones and cut the meat into pieces. In a food processor, coarsely chop the okra, carrots, onion and celery. Place the chicken, chopped vegetables, and broth in a large saucepan. Add the sugar, salt, pepper, celery seed and bouillon cube. Cook for one hour. Add the V-8 juice, peas and corn. Cook an additional 30 minutes.

Yields: 16 servings

Jackie Brown

♦ BRUNSWICK STEW ♦

A dear family friend made this stew for our family,
when we gathered for Granny's funeral. This stew is
a lot of work, but is well worth the effort!

6 to 7	pound slightly fat hen or 2 plump fryers
1 1/2	pounds onions, chopped
1 to 2	tablespoons all-purpose flour
	Cooking bag(s)
1	pound ground chuck
3	pounds potatoes, peeled and sliced
1	pound dried butter beans or 1 package frozen baby lima beans
3	28-ounce cans tomatoes
1	stick margarine or butter
1	14-ounce bottle ketchup
	Sugar, salt and pepper to taste
5	ounces Worcestershire sauce
2	16-ounce cans creamed corn
	Instant potatoes as needed to thicken, optional

Day 1: Preheat oven to 350 degrees. In a cooking bag, place the chicken, onions and flour. Close bag with the tie provided. Place the bag in a pan at least two inches deep. The bag should not hang over the sides. Make six 1/2 inch slits in the top of the bag. Bake at 350 degrees for 1 1/2 to 2 hours. To open, cut or slit the top of the bag carefully. Strain the broth and reserve. Refrigerate the whole chicken and the broth.

If using butter beans, pick over, rinse and soak the beans in warm water to cover over night. Cook in water to cover until tender, one to two hours. Refrigerate.

Day 2: In a skillet, brown the ground chuck and drain. Cook the butter beans in water to cover until tender, approximately 1 1/2 to 2 hours. In a medium sauce pan, cook the potatoes in water, until tender, and then mash.

Discard the skin and remove the meat from the bones of the refrigerated chicken. Chop the chicken and onions. In a large stock pot, combine the chicken, chicken broth, ground chuck, and tomatoes. Bring to a boil. Reduce heat and simmer for one hour.

Add the chopped onions and cooked butter beans (or lima beans), stirring gently to blend ingredients. Continue to simmer over low heat. Add the mashed potatoes. Stir in sugar, salt, and pepper to taste, along with 2 1/2 ounces of Worcestershire sauce. Add the creamed corn, margarine and ketchup. If the stew is not thick enough, add small amounts of instant potatoes, cooking after each addition until done, then adding more if necessary. To prevent sticking or burning, scoop the stew into two crock pots and cook on low for five or more hours.

Before serving, stir in remaining Worcestershire sauce. This stew freezes well.

Yields: 20 to 24 servings

Eleanor Helms

♦ HOMEMADE ♦
VEGETABLE SOUP

4	*large potatoes, peeled and diced*
5	*carrots, peeled and diced*
3	*stalks celery, diced*
1	*large onion, diced*
1/4 to 1/2	*teaspoon onion salt*
1/4 to 1/2	*teaspoon celery salt*
1 1/2	*16-ounce packages frozen okra*
1 1/2	*16-ounce packages frozen corn*
1 1/2	*16-ounce packages frozen lima beans*
3	*14-ounce cans tomatoes, chopped*
1 1/2	*46-ounce cans V-8 juice*
1 to 1 1/2	*pounds roast beef, cooked and chopped*
1/2 to 3/4	*cup beef gravy*
2	*tablespoons Worcestershire sauce*
1	*tablespoon sugar*
	Salt and pepper to taste

In a large Dutch oven, combine the potatoes, carrots, onion, onion and celery salts, okra, corn, lima beans, tomatoes, and V-8 juice. Mix well. Add the beef, gravy, Worcestershire sauce and sugar. Add the salt and pepper to taste. Bring to a boil. Reduce to medium-low heat and cook for 1 1/2 to 2 hours.

Yields: 12 to 14 servings

Eleanor Helms

◆VEGETABLE BEEF SOUP◆

1	pound lean stew beef, chopped
1	onion, chopped
2	carrots, sliced
1	large potato, cubed
1	gallon water
1	large package frozen okra
1	large package frozen mixed vegetables
1	can green peas
1	can creamed corn
1	beef bouillon cube
1	tablespoon salt
1	teaspoon pepper
1/4	cup sugar
1	46-ounce can V-8 juice

Cut off any fat on the beef and brown. Chop the onion, carrots and potato in a food processor. In a Dutch oven, combine the beef, chopped vegetables and water. Add the bouillon, salt, pepper and sugar. Cook for one hour. Add the V-8 juice, corn and peas. Cook for 30 additional minutes.

Yields: 12 to 14 servings

Jackie Brown

◆ SPICY ◆
VEGETABLE SOUP

1	16-ounce can tomatoes
1	quart water
2	pounds boneless beef chuck roast, cut into 1 inch cubes
1	beef shin bone, optional
1	teaspoon salt
1	teaspoon pepper
1	cup chopped celery, including some tops
1	tablespoon minced fresh parsley
1	bay leaf
2	16-ounce cans V-8 juice
1	10-ounce package frozen green beans
2	cups sliced carrots
1	12-ounce can corn, drained
1 1/2	cups thinly-sliced onion
1 to 2	teaspoons mixed dried herbs (basil, thyme, oregano, marjoram)
1	teaspoon Worcestershire sauce
2	beef bouillon cubes

Drain the tomatoes, reserving liquid, and place in a 6-quart sauce pan. Add the water, meat, shin bone, salt, pepper, celery, parsley, and bay leaf. Cover and simmer for one hour. Add the V-8 juice, tomatoes, beans, carrots, corn, onion, herbs, Worcestershire sauce, bouillon cubes, and additional water if soup seems too thick. Simmer uncovered for 1 to 1 1/2 hours. Remove the bone, bay leaf, and celery tops. Cool and refrigerate soup. Remove any fat congealed on top. Reheat for serving.

Yields: 10 to 12 servings

Deborah Alston

◆ Paul's Special Soup ◆

1/2	pound lean pork sausage
1 1/4	pounds lean stew beef, cut into bite-size pieces
1	large onion, chopped
1	46-ounce can V-8 juice
3	14 1/2-ounce cans stewed tomatoes (with celery, peppers, onions)
1	teaspoon basil
1	teaspoon oregano
1	teaspoon garlic powder
1	teaspoon pepper
1	teaspoon Beau Monde or salt
5	large to medium potatoes, diced
1	16-ounce can sliced carrots, drained, or 4 fresh carrots, sliced and cooked separately
1	16-ounce can baby lima beans, drained
1	16-ounce can whole kernel golden sweet corn, drained
1	large wedge cabbage, cut-up (optional)
1	4 1/2-ounce can mushroom pieces, drained (optional)
1	16-ounce can sliced okra, drained (optional)

In large pot, brown the sausage and stew beef. Drain the fat. Add the onions and saute. In food blender, pour stewed tomatoes and pulse. Add the V-8 juice, stewed tomatoes, and seasoning to meat mixture. Heat slowly until soup bubbles; stir often to avoid scorching. Add the potatoes and simmer with lid on for 1 1/2-2 hours, stirring occasionally. If cabbage is used, cabbage can be cooked with meat and potatoes or cooked separately. When meat is tender and potatoes are cooked, add canned vegetables. Stir to mix all vegetables and bring back to a simmer for a few minutes.

Yields: 24 servings

Paul Allen

♦ SIMPLY ♦
DELICIOUS SOUP

This is my husband's favorite soup!
It's very easy to prepare and is a meal in itself.

1   large onion, chopped
1   pound lean ground beef
2   cans cream of celery soup
1   46-ounce can V-8 juice
2   cups grated carrots (3-4 carrots)

Brown beef and saute onions in large pan. Add the soup, V-8 juice and carrots to the beef. Cook over low heat for 1 hour. Stir soup frequently to keep from sticking.

Yields: 8 servings

Margaret Young

◆ CABBAGE ◆
AND BEEF SOUP

1	pound lean ground beef
1/2	teaspoon garlic salt
1/4	teaspoon garlic powder
1/4	teaspoon ground black pepper
2	celery stalks, chopped
1	16-ounce can kidney beans, undrained
1/2	medium head cabbage, chopped
1	28-ounce can tomatoes, chopped and liquid reserved
1	tomato can filled with water
4	beef bouillon cubes
	Chopped fresh parsley, optional

In a Dutch oven, brown the beef. Add the garlic salt and powder, pepper, celery, kidney beans, cabbage, tomatoes, water and bouillon cubes. Bring the soup to a boil. Reduce the heat and simmer for approximately one hour. Add the chopped parsley as garnish when served.

Yields: 10 to 12 servings

Pat Rush

♦ HUEVOS RANCHEROS ♦

1	*pound bacon, cut into small pieces*
1/2 to 1	*package frozen hash brown potatoes*
	Pepper
	Seasoned salt
	Salt (optional)
	Tabasco sauce
2	*eggs per person*
1	*cup grated cheddar cheese*
1	*medium onion, chopped*
1	*jar salsa sauce*

In a large frying pan with a cover, cook the bacon. Drain the bacon and set aside. Leave a little grease in the pan and fry the hash browns and onions. Season with pepper, seasoned salt, salt and tabasco sauce. Cook until golden brown.

Crack eggs on top of hash browns; keep the eggs away from the edge of pan. Sprinkle on the cheese. Sprinkle salsa over the cheese. Sprinkle bacon on the salsa.

Cover and cook until eggs are done to taste.

Yields: up to 8 servings

Debbie Brown

◆ Mexican Quiche ◆

If you like quiche but are watching your cholesterol, you will enjoy this recipe. It's easy to make and freezes nicely.

1/3	*pound low fat sausage (optional)*
1	*cup shredded Monterey Jack cheese with jalapenos*
1	*cup reduced-cholesterol egg substitute*
1/2	*cup milk*
1/3	*cup chopped green pepper*
1/3	*cup chopped scallions*
1/2 to 3/4	*teaspoon salt*
1	*9-inch dish pie crust*

Preheat oven to 475 degrees. Brown the sausage and drain well. In a bowl, combine the cheese, eggs, milk, green pepper, scallions and salt. Add the sausage. Stir until blended. Pour into an unbaked 9-inch deep dish pie crust.

Bake at 475 degrees for 15 minutes; lower heat to 325 degrees and bake an additonal 20 minutes or until set.

Yields: 6 servings

Karen Harris

◆ EGG BRUNCH ◆

2	slices bacon, cut up
1	small jar dried beef, cut coarsely
1	3-ounce can sliced mushrooms
2	tablespoons butter
1/4	cup all-purpose flour
2	cups milk
	Pepper to taste
8	eggs
1/2	cup evaporated milk
2	tablespoons butter
	Fresh mushrooms (optional)

Preheat oven to 275 degrees. Saute the bacon until almost done. Add the dried beef, mushrooms, and two tablespoons margarine. Stir in the flour and then milk. Add pepper to taste. Stir until thickened and set aside.

Mix the eggs with the evaporated milk and soft scramble in the butter.

Grease a shallow casserole dish. Place a small amount of sauce in the bottom. Layer half of the eggs, then half of the sauce. Layer remaining eggs, then remaining sauce. Garnish top with mushrooms, if desired.

Heat covered at 275 degrees for one hour. Dish may be prepared in advance, refrigerated and heated when needed.

Yields: 6 servings

Martha Helms

♦ Salads and Fruits ♦

Pat and Margaret Allen

The girls are riding "Tiny," the horse, in 1936.

My mother, Margaret, and her sister Pat are pictured here on a pony at the family's "farm" on Willow Oak Drive, where they led a life of fun and adventure. They collected fireflies and took them to the movie theater, where they would let the flies go and watch the audience react to the sudden sparks of light. They sewed socks together to form a tube, stuffed it, then laid the "snake" across the road and watched as cars screeched to a stop and riders fled from their car. They have great tales about neighborhood fish fries that were held in a small wooden house behind a neighbor's home. Years later, Margaret purchased the building and moved it to our backyard to be my treasured playhouse.

Margaret's shy smile hides the mind of an engineer. My husband claims that Margaret is one of the few people who can instantly grasp the intricacies of a rented "U-Haul" tow bar. Bless her, too, for that sense of history that made her save all the precious things that made my childhood sweet. Thanks for keeping my Barbie dolls, Mom.

Pat's stern look in this photograph hides the biggest heart in the family. Pat and her husband Bob have many of Granny's selfless ways. They have done a thousand things to make people's lives better, quietly and modestly. Growing up with Granny's example for how we should care for each other—and those less fortunate—left its wonderful mark on all the children, especially Aunt Pat.

♦ HEAVENLY ♦
ORANGE FLUFF

Gelatin:

2	3-ounce packages orange gelatin
2	cups hot water
1	small can frozen orange juice, undiluted
2	small cans mandarin oranges, drained
1	large can crushed pineapple (including juice)

Topping:

1	package instant lemon pudding
1	cup milk
1/2	pint whipping cream

To prepare gelatin: Mix the gelatin with hot water until dissolved. Add the orange juice and let mixture cool. Add the oranges and pineapple to the mixture. Pour into a 13x11-inch dish and refrigerate.

To prepare topping: Beat the pudding with milk until slightly firm. Whip the cream and fold into the pudding. Spread the topping on the gelatin. Cut into squares and serve on lettuce.

Yields: 12 servings

Margaret Young

◆ ORANGE ◆
BUTTERMILK SALAD

1	8 1/2-ounce can crushed pineapple with syrup
1	6-ounce package orange Jello
2	cups buttermilk
1	8-ounce carton frozen whipped topping, thawed
1/2	cup chopped pecans

In a large saucepan, bring the pineapple and syrup to a boil. Remove the saucepan from the heat and stir in the Jello. Cool to room temperature. Stir in the buttermilk. Fold in the whipped topping and pecans and pour mixture into an 8-cup mold. Chill for four hours or overnight.

Yields: 6 to 8 servings

Pat Rush

◆ SOUR CHERRY SALAD ◆

1	*package plain gelatin*
1/4	*cup cold water*
	Juice and rind of one lemon
	Juice and rind of one orange
1	*large can sour cherries, drained with juice reserved*
1/2	*cup sugar*
1	*6-ounce package lemon Jello*
3/4	*cup pecans*
1	*large can crushed pineapple with juice*
	Red food coloring

Dissolve the gelatin in cold water, according to the package directions, and set aside.

Bring to a boil the lemon, orange and cherry juices. Add the sugar and Jello. Let the mixture cool until the consistency of unbeaten egg whites. Add the gelatin, cherries, pecans and pineapple. Pour into a 6 1/2-cup mold and refrigerate.

Yields: 6 to 8 servings

Eleanor Helms

◆ Apricot Salad ◆

2   *3-ounce packages apricot Jello*
1   *8-ounce can crushed pineapple*
2   *cups buttermilk*
1   *cup chopped pecans*

Heat the Jello and pineapple until the Jello dissolves. Set mixture aside to cool.

Fold the buttermilk and pecans into the Jello mixture. Pour the Jello mixture into a 6 1/2-cup mold and refrigerate.

Yields: 6 to 8 servings

Margaret Young

◆ APRICOT CHEESE ◆ DELIGHT SALAD

Salad:

1	17-ounce can apricots, drained with juice reserved
1	large can crushed pineapple, drained with juice reserved
1	cup miniature marshmallows
2	3-ounce packages orange flavored gelatin
2	cups hot water

Topping:

1/2	cup sugar
3	tablespoons all-purpose flour
1	egg, slightly beaten
2	tablespoons margarine or butter
1	cup whipping cream (whipped) or Cool Whip
3/4	cup grated cheese

To prepare the salad: Drain the fruit, keeping the reserved apricot and pineapple juices separate. Chill the apricots and pineapple. Dissolve the gelatin in hot water and add one cup of apricot juice. Fold in the apricots, pineapple and marshmallows. Chill until firm.

To prepare the topping: Combine the sugar and flour. Blend in the egg and margarine Add one cup of pineapple juice and cook over low heat, stirring constantly until thickened. Let cool thoroughly. Fold in whipped cream and spread over the congealed salad. Sprinkle with cheese and chill.

Yields: 12 servings

Jackie Brown

◆ Strawberry Salad ◆

2   *3-ounce packages strawberry Jello*
1   *cup boiling water*
2   *packages frozen strawberries, thawed*
1   *20-ounce can crushed pineapple*
2 to 3   *bananas, mashed*
1   *cup chopped pecans*
2   *cups sour cream*

Combine the Jello and water and stir until dissolved. Add the strawberries, pineapple, bananas and pecans. Pour half of the mixture into a 9x9-inch pan and chill until firm. Spread the sour cream over the firm mixture. Pour the remaining Jello mixture over the congealed salad. Refrigerate for at least four hours.

Yields: 8 servings

Jackie Brown

◆ Pistachio Salad ◆

1   *16-ounce can crushed pineapple*
1   *3-ounce package pistachio instant pudding*
1   *cup miniature marshmallows*
1   *9-ounce carton Cool Whip*

Combine the pineapple, pudding, marshmallows, and whipped cream. Pour into a 9x9-inch pan and refrigerate for at least two hours.

Yields: 6 servings

Deborah Alston

◆ MIXED FRUIT SALAD ◆

3   bananas, sliced
3   apples, peeled, cored and sliced
3   oranges, sliced
1/2   pound red or white grapes, sliced in half
1/2   fresh pineapple, sliced in bite-sized chunks
1   cup orange juice
    Sugar to taste, optional

In a medium bowl, combine the bananas, apples, oranges, grapes, and orange juice. Add sugar to taste and chill.

Yields: 6 to 8 servings

Margaret Young

◆ FROZEN FRUIT SALAD ◆

2 1/2   cups sour cream
2 1/2   tablespoons lemon juice
1   cup sugar
1/8   teaspoon salt
1   cup drained crushed pineapple
1/2   cup chopped nuts
1/4   cup chopped maraschino cherries
1   large banana, chopped
    Mandarin orange slices, optional

Combine all the ingredients in a large bowl. Pour into paper cupcake cups in muffin pans and freeze. When frozen, remove from pans and freeze in storage bags.

Yields: 18 servings

Deborah Alston

◆ 24-HOUR SALAD ◆

Colorful and festive. Looks great
served in glass bowl.

1	20-ounce can pineapple tidbits (2 1/2 cups)
1	16-ounce can pitted white cherries or 1 can fruit cocktail
3	egg yolks
2	tablespoons vinegar
2	tablespoons sugar
	Dash salt
1	tablespoon butter or margarine
2	medium oranges, peeled and diced or one can mandarin oranges
2	cups tiny marshmallows or 16 large marshmallows, cut in eighths
1	cup whipping cream, whipped

Drain the pineapple, reserving two tablespoons syrup. Drain the cherries. In the top of a double boiler, beat egg yolks slightly. Add the reserved pineapple syrup, vinegar, sugar, salt, and butter. Place over hot, not boiling water; cook, stirring constantly, until mixture thickens slightly and barely coats a spoon (about 12 minutes). Cool to room temperature.

Combine the well-drained oranges, pineapple, cherries, and marshmallows. Pour the custard over the fruit and mix gently. Fold in the whipped cream and pour into a serving bowl. Cover and chill 24 hours. Garnish with fresh fruit.

Yields: 6 to 8 servings

Margaret Young

♦ FRUIT ♦
COCKTAIL SALAD

1   *can fruit cocktail, drained*
2   *cans mandarin oranges, drained*
1   *cup sour cream*
1/2 *package tiny marshmallows*

Combine all ingredients and refrigerate at least three hours.

Yields: 6 to 8 servings

Margaret Young

♦ CRANBERRY SALAD ♦

1   *3-ounce package orange flavored gelatin*
1   *3-ounce package cherry flavored gelatin*
2   *cups hot water*
2   *cups coarsely ground raw cranberries*
2   *oranges, one peeled, one unpeeled, coarsely chopped in blender*
1/2 *cup chopped nuts*
1/2 *cup chopped celery*
1   *cup sugar*

Dissolve the gelatins in hot water, stirring until completely smooth. Cool to consistency of unbeaten egg whites. Combine the cranberries, oranges, nuts, celery and sugar and mix with the gelatin. Pour into a 9-inch mold and refrigerate.

Yields: 6 to 8 servings

Margaret Young

♦ HAM AND ♦
CHEESE SALAD

1	8-ounce package corkscrew pasta
1/2	pound cooked ham, cut into 2-inch strips
1	cup broccoli flowerets
1	cup frozen green peas, thawed
1	small yellow squash, thinly sliced
1	small red pepper, cut into thin strips
4	ounces Swiss cheese, cubed
1/2	cup mayonnaise
2	tablespoons Dijon mustard
1/4	cup milk
1/4	cup grated Parmesan cheese

Cook and drain pasta; rinse pasta with cold water and drain again. Combine the pasta with the ham, broccoli, peas, squash, red pepper, and Swiss cheese.

Separately, combine mayonnaise, mustard and milk. Stir well. Toss the mayonnaise mixture with the vegetable mixture. Sprinkle with Parmesan cheese. Cover and chill for two hours.

Yields: 6 servings

Martha Helms

♦ FROZEN ♦
TURKEY-VEGETABLE SALAD

3   *envelopes (2 tablespoons) unflavored gelatin*
1/2   *cup cold water*
2   *10 3/4-ounce cans condensed cream of celery soup*
4   *cups finely diced cooked turkey*
2   *10-ounce packages frozen mixed vegetables, cooked*
       and drained
1   *cup Miracle Whip (do not use mayonnaise)*

Line two 8-inch square pans with aluminum foil, allowing enough extra foil to fold over the top. Soften the gelatin in the water. Heat the soup and gelatin, stirring until the gelatin is dissolved. Add the turkey, vegetables and Miracle Whip, folding all together gently. Divide the mixture between two 9x9-inch pans. Fold the foil over top and freeze until firm.

Remove the frozen blocks from the pans, fold and seal foil tightly, label, and return to freezer. Before serving, place frozen blocks in the refrigerator and thaw completely.

Yields: 12 servings

Margaret Young

♦ KATHRYN'S ♦
CHICKEN SALAD

Fabulously different--always a success.

2	tablespoons margarine or butter
2	tablespoons vinegar
2	tablespoons prepared mustard
2	teaspoons sugar
2	eggs, lightly beaten
1	teaspoon salt
1	teaspoon pepper
2	cups chopped chicken
1/2	cup chopped celery
	Sweet pickle juice
	Accent
	Mayonnaise

Combine the margarine, vinegar, mustard, sugar, eggs, salt and pepper in a heavy saucepan. Stir over low heat until it thickens. Pour the mixture over chicken. Add the celery, pickle juice, Accent and mayonnaise to the consistency you prefer. Chill overnight.

Yields: 6 servings

Deborah Alston

♦ CHICKEN SALAD ♦

1	whole chicken
2	stalks celery, chopped
1/2	cup chopped pecans
1/2	cup Miracle Whip salad dressing
	Salt and pepper to taste

Place the chicken in pan with water to cover. Cook the chicken over medium-high heat 35 to 45 minutes, until the meat is falling from the bones. Remove the skin and discard. Remove the chicken meat and chop. Add the chopped celery, pecans and Miracle Whip. Mix thoroughly. Add the salt and pepper to taste.

Yields: 6 to 8 servings

Margaret Young

◆ BAKED ◆
CHICKEN SALAD

3	whole chicken breasts, boiled and chopped
1	10-ounce can cream of chicken soup
1	cup chopped celery
2	tablespoons minced onion
1/2	teaspoon salt
1/2	teaspoon pepper
1	tablespoon lemon juice
3/4	cup mayonnaise
3	hard boiled eggs, chopped
2	cups crushed potato chips
1/2	cup chopped almonds, optional

Preheat oven to 450 degrees. Mix the chicken, soup, celery, onion, salt, pepper, lemon juice, mayonnaise, and eggs. Top with chips and almonds.

Bake at 450 degrees for 15 minutes.

Yields: 10 to 12 servings

Jackie Brown

◆ New England ◆ Cole Slaw

1   cup mayonnaise
1/2   cup sour cream
1/4   cup extra virgin olive oil
2   tablespoons Dijon mustard
2   tablespoons honey
2   tablespoons red wine vinegar
5 to 6   drops hot sauce
1   medium cabbage, shredded
1   large carrot, shredded
1/2   green pepper, chopped
1   green onion, chopped
1   cucumber, sliced
         Fresh ground pepper
         Celery seed

Combine the mayonnaise, sour cream, olive oil, mustard, honey, vinegar and hot sauce in a jar and shake well.

Mix the cabbage and carrots in a large bowl. Add the green pepper, green onion and cucumber in the quantities you desire. Add mayonnaise mixture and toss. Season with fresh ground pepper and celery seed.

Yields: 10 to 12 servings

Martha Helms

♦ MARINATED ♦
COLE SLAW

1	tablespoon salt
2	cups sugar
2	cups vinegar
2	cups water
3	pounds cabbage, shredded or chopped
2	onions, chopped
2	green peppers, chopped
2	tablespoons mustard seeds
1	small can pimento, cut up

Combine the salt, sugar, vinegar and water in a small bowl. In a large bowl, combine the cabbage, onions, green peppers, mustard seeds, and pimento. Pour the vinegar mixture over the slaw and toss. Refrigerate at least 24 hours before eating. Can be refrigerated for up to a month.

Yields: 36 servings

Jackie Brown

◆ 20-MINUTE ◆ POTATO SALAD

2   *pounds Idaho potatoes, peeled and diced*
1   *medium green pepper, cut into strips*
1   *medium onion, chopped*
2   *celery stalks, chopped*
1   *cup sour cream*
1   *cup low-fat mayonnaise*
     Salt and pepper to taste

Cook the potatoes in boiling water for 10 to 12 minutes, or until tender. Drain and let cool. Add the green pepper, onion and celery to the potatoes and toss. In a small bowl, combine the sour cream and mayonnaise and mix well. Add the sour cream mixture to the potatoes and toss Salt and pepper the salad to taste. Mix lightly and refrigerate.

Yields: 6 servings

Margaret Young

◆ POTATO SALAD ◆

6	*cups potatoes, peeled, diced and cooked*
1/3	*cup bottled Italian Dressing*
3/4	*cup diced celery*
1/3	*cup green onion*
4	*hard-boiled eggs*
3/4 to 1	*cup mayonnaise*
1/3 to 1/2	*cup sour cream*
1 1/2	*teaspoons horseradish, optional*

Cook the potatoes over medium-high heat for approximately 20 minutes, until tender. Marinate the cooked potatoes in Italian dressing for two to three hours. Add the celery, onion, eggs, mayonnaise, sour cream, and horseradish. Refrigerate before serving.

Yields: 10 to 12 servings

Eleanor Helms

♦ BROCCOLI SALAD ♦

2	bunches broccoli, approximately 2 1/4 cups
10	slices bacon, cooked, drained and crumbled
1	large red onion
1/4	cup dark raisins
1/4	cup golden raisins
1	cup mayonnaise
1/4	cup sugar
2	tablespoons cider vinegar
1/2	teaspoon black pepper
1/3	cup celery, chopped
1/2	cup toasted sunflower seeds, optional

Cut the broccoli florets into smaller than bite-size pieces. Cut off the tough outer layer of the stalks and chop the tender part into small pieces. This can be done the day before and refrigerated in a plastic bag.

Slice the onion lengthwise and cut into julienne strips. In a large bowl, combine the broccoli, onion strips, raisins, and bacon.

In a small bowl, whisk together the mayonnaise, sugar, vinegar and pepper. Combine the dressing with the vegetables, and refrigerate for at least two hours before serving. Toss the salad at least once while refrigerating the salad. Top with sunflower seeds, if desired.

Yields: 10 to 12 servings

Karen Harris

♦ CAULIFLOWER ♦ CRUNCHY SALAD

1	head lettuce, chopped
1	head cauliflower, thinly sliced
1	large red onion, thinly sliced and chopped
1	tablespoon sugar
1	pound bacon, cooked, drained and crumbled
1/2 to 3/4	cup mayonnaise
	Grated Parmesan cheese

Place a layer of lettuce in a large salad bowl. Add a thin layer of cauliflower over lettuce. Put a thin layer of sliced onion over the cauliflower. Sprinkle with sugar and then bacon. Repeat the layers of lettuce, cauliflower, onion, sugar and bacon. Top the salad with mayonnaise. Sprinkle with Parmesan cheese. Refrigerate for at least two hours. Toss the salad just before serving.

Yields: 6 to 8 servings

Margaret Young

◆ LAYERED ◆
SPINACH SALAD

One of our holiday favorites!

1	package fresh spinach, washed and shredded
1	10-ounce package frozen green peas, cooked and drained
5 to 6	slices bacon, cooked, drained and crumbled
2	hard-boiled eggs, chopped
1	small green onion, chopped
1	8-ounce carton sour cream
1	cup mayonnaise
	Grated Parmesan cheese

In large salad bowl, place layers of spinach, peas, bacon, eggs, and onion. In small bowl, mix the sour cream and mayonnaise. Spread the dressing mixture over the top of the salad. Sprinkle with Parmesan cheese. Refrigerate until ready to serve. Toss just before serving.

Yields: 6 to 8 servings

Margaret Young

♦ "QUICK" ♦
CAESAR SALAD

1	*head of Romaine lettuce, washed and shredded*
1/2	*cup fresh cheddar cheese*
1	*cup Caesar salad croutons*
	Caesar salad dressing

In salad bowl, combine lettuce, cheddar cheese and croutons. Add the Caesar salad dressing and toss.

Yields: 6 servings

Jackie Brown

♦ CREAMY ♦
ITALIAN DRESSING

1	*cup mayonnaise*
1/2	*small onion, chopped*
2	*tablespoons red wine vinegar or balsamic vinegar*
1	*tablespoon sugar*
1/4	*teaspoon salt*
1/4	*teaspoon garlic salt or garlic powder*
3/4	*teaspoon Italian seasoning*
1/8	*teaspoon pepper*

Blend above ingredients in a blender for 15 to 30 seconds. Refrigerate before serving.

Yields: approximately 1 1/4 cups

Margaret Young

♦ VINAIGRETTE ♦
DRESSING

1   clove garlic, minced
1   tablespoon Dijon mustard
1   tablespoon red vinegar
1/2   teaspoon salt
3   tablespoons lemon juice
11   tablespoons extra virgin olive oil

Combine the garlic, mustard, vinegar, salt, lemon juice, and olive oil and mix well. Refrigerate.

Yields: approximately 1 cup

Margaret Young

♦ SPINACH ♦
SALAD DRESSING

1/2   *cup honey*
1/4   *cup water*
1/4   *cup wine vinegar*
1/4   *cup vegetable oil*
1   *teaspoon soy sauce*
      Pepper to taste

Combine the honey, water, vinegar, oil, soy sauce and pepper. Mix well and refrigerate.

Yields: approximately 1 1/4 cups

Margaret Young

♦MARINATED BROCCOLI♦

2 or 3 *bunches broccoli, trimmed and chopped*
1   *cup cider vinegar*
1   *tablespoon dill seed*
1   *tablespoon salt*
1   *tablespoon Accent*
1   *teaspoon garlic salt*
1   *cup oil*
      Cherry tomatoes

Combine the vinegar, dill seed, salt, Accent, garlic salt and oil. Marinate the broccoli in the oil mixture overnight. Serve in a large bowl garnished with cherry tomatoes.

Yields: approximately 8 to 10 cups

Margaret Young

◆ FRESH VEGETABLE ◆ MARINADE

4	*stalks fresh broccoli*
8	*large fresh mushrooms, sliced*
1	*medium-size green pepper, chopped*
3	*stalks celery, chopped*
1	*small head cauliflower, broken into flowerets*
1	*cup sugar*
2	*teaspoons dry mustard*
1	*teaspoon salt*
1/2	*cup vinegar*
1 1/2	*cups vegetable oil*
1	*small onion, grated*
2	*tablespoons poppy seed*

Remove flowerets from broccoli and cut into bite-size pieces. Reserve stalks for other use. Combine the flowerets, mushrooms, pepper, celery, and cauliflower; toss lightly.

Combine the sugar, mustard, salt, vinegar, oil, onion and poppy seeds. Mix well, and pour over vegetables. Chill for at least three hours.

Yields: 10 to 12 servings

Eleanor Helms

◆ Pineapple Dressing ◆ for Fruit Salad

3   whole eggs
2   egg yolks
3/4 to 1   cup pineapple juice
3/4   cup sugar
1/3   cup lemon juice

Beat together the eggs and yolks. Combine with the pineapple juice, sugar and lemon juice. Cook over low heat, stirring constantly with a wire whisk, until thickened. Cool completely. Dressing will keep refrigerated for up to two weeks.

Yields: 2 cups

Deborah Alston

◆ Spiced Apples ◆

2   Golden Delicious apples, peeled and cored
1   tablespoon margarine or butter
2   teaspoons granulated sugar
1/2   teaspoon ground cinnamon

Slice the apples into 12 wedges. In a skillet, heat the margarine over medium-high heat. Add the apples. Sprinkle with sugar and cinnamon. Cook about six minutes, stirring occasionally until apples are lightly browned and just tender.

Yields: 4 to 6 servings

Deborah Alston

♦ PEACH CRISPS ♦

Delicious! Can serve as a healthy
dessert or as breakfast fruit.

6	large peaches, about 3 pounds
1/4	cup sugar plus 3 tablespoons
1/3	cup all-purpose flour plus 2 tablespoons
3	tablespoons light corn-oil margarine
1/8	teaspoon ground cinnamon

Preheat oven to 400 degrees. Peel and thinly slice peaches. In large bowl, toss peaches with 1/4 cup sugar and 2 tablespoons flour. Spoon the peach mixture into five 8-ounce ramekins or custard cups.

In small bowl, combine the margarine, cinnamon, 1/3 cup flour, and 3 tablespoons sugar until mixture resembles coarse crumbs. Sprinkle the flour mixture on peaches.

Place the ramekins in a jelly-roll pan for easier handling. Bake at 400 degrees for 25 to 30 minutes, until peach mixture is bubbly and crumb topping is golden brown. Serve warm.

Yields: 5 servings

Deborah Alston

◆ CARIBBEAN PEARS ◆

5	pears, partially ripened
1 1/2	cups orange juice
3/4	cup packed brown sugar
10 to 15	whole cloves
	Mint leaves
1/2	teaspoon allspice
2 to 3	cinnamon sticks, broken in 1/2-inch pieces
2	tablespoons triple sec

Preheat oven to 350 degrees. Peel, halve, and with melon baller, remove the core of the pears. Place halves, cut side down, in a 13x9-inch baking dish. Combine the juice, sugar, spices, and triple sec and pour over the pears. Bake at 350 degrees for 50 to 60 minutes, basting occasionally.

To serve, place the pear on the plate and slice lengthwise into three segments, but not slicing all of the way to the top. Decorate with cinnamon sticks to resemble stem and mint leaves. Spoon sauce over pears.

Yields: 10 servings

Deborah Alston

◆ BREAD ◆

Jackie and Eleanor Allen

*Eleanor, Granny's youngest daughter, has been at it again.
She made Jackie pout by taking her firetruck.*

Granny's youngest daughters, Jackie and Eleanor were always up to something. There's an old family story about a dear neighbor named Mr. Busbin, who often visited the Allen home. On one occasion, Eleanor spotted Mr. Busbin in the den. Knowing that Jackie didn't have any clothes on, she brought Mr. Busbin back to the bedroom. Hearing them approach, Jackie darted under the bed. Eleanor told Mr. Busbin, "Look under the bed, Mr. Busbin." Jackie jumped up from under the bed, naked as a jay bird. "Look up, Mr. Busbin, look up." To Jackie's horror, the poor man kept it up for a while, trying to humor Eleanor. Jackie and Eleanor still giggle when they tell this story. They've concluded that Mr. Busbin's eyesight was so poor, even if he had caught a glimpse of Jackie, he still wouldn't have known she was in her birthday suit.

Jackie and Eleanor have always been a source of laughter and wit for the family. Over the years, they have been very close and can, to this day, communicate with rapid phrases, words and partial sentences that leave others baffled. Dad claims that the four sisters—when Jackie and Eleanor are in their best form—can actually carry on four conversations at once with full comprehension. My husband is still amazed when he witnesses this phenomenon.

◆ SOUR CREAM ◆ DINNER ROLLS

*These rolls are wonderful! They disappear
quickly at family gatherings.*

1	cup sour cream
1/2	cup sugar
1	teaspoon salt
1	stick margarine, melted
2	tablespoons margarine, melted
1/2	cup lukewarm water
2	packages active dry yeast
2	eggs
4	cups all-purpose flour, unsifted

Scald the sour cream. Stir in the sugar, salt, and the stick of margarine. Cool to lukewarm.

Put lukewarm water into large bowl, sprinkle in the yeast, and stir until dissolved. Add the lukewarm sour cream mixture, eggs, and flour. Mix until well blended. Cover tightly with plastic wrap and refrigerate over night.

Preheat oven to 375 degrees. Divide dough into quarters. Flour board lightly and roll one part of the dough out until it is about 1/4 inch thick. Cut the dough with a round cutter or a glass. Brush each roll with the remaining melted margarine, fold over, seal edges and place closely together on greased pan. Let the rolls rise 45 minutes. Bake at 375 degrees for 12 to 15 minutes.

Yields: 48 rolls

Margaret Young

◆ REFRIGERATOR ◆ POTATO ROLLS

1	package instant mashed potatoes (enough for 4 servings)
4 1/2 to 4 3/4	cups all-purpose flour
1	package active dry yeast
1	cup milk
1/2	cup vegetable shortening
1/2	cup sugar
1	teaspoon salt
2	eggs

Prepare the mashed potatoes according to package directions and set aside. In a large bowl, thoroughly stir together two cups of flour and the yeast.

In a saucepan, heat the milk, shortening, sugar and salt until warm (115 to 120 degrees), stirring constantly to melt shortening. Stir the potatoes into the milk mixture. Add the milk mixture to the dry mixture. Add the eggs. Beat at low speed for 1/2 minute, scraping the sides of bowl constantly. Beat three minutes at high speed. By hand, stir in enough remaining flour to make a soft dough. Place in a greased bowl, turning once to grease surface, and cover. Refrigerate the dough for several hours or up to one week.

Make into rolls as needed. Preheat oven to 375 degrees. Place on greased baking pan, and let dough rise about 45 minutes (until double in size). Bake at 375 degrees for approximately 25 minutes.

Yields: 48 rolls

Margaret Young

♦ WHITE BREAD ♦

3/4	cup water
2	cups white bread flour
1	tablespoon dry milk
1 1/2	tablespoons sugar
1	teaspoon salt
1	tablespoon margarine or butter, cut up
1 1/2	teaspoons active dry yeast

To bake in a bread machine: Place the above ingredients in the bread pan and place pan in bread machine. Set the machine on the regular time cycle set for light crust. When the baking cycle is finished, remove bread from machine immediately and allow to cool before serving.

Suggested use: For low fat croutons, lightly butter bread slices, cube and bake at 350 degrees until crisp.

Yields: 1-pound loaf

Karen Harris

♦Honey Wheat Bread♦

3/4   cup lukewarm water
1 1/2   cups white bread flour
1/2   cup wheat bread flour
1   tablespoon dry milk
1   tablespoon honey
1   teaspoon salt
1   tablespoon margarine or butter, cut up
1 1/2   teaspoons active dry yeast

To bake in a bread machine: Place the above ingredients in the bread pan and place pan in bread machine. Set the machine on whole wheat cycle. When the baking cycle is finished, remove bread from machine immediately and allow to cool before serving.

Yields: 1-pound loaf

Karen Harris

♦Louise Rush's Biscuits♦

4   cups self-rising flour, sifted
3/4   cup vegetable shortening
1   cup buttermilk

Preheat oven to 450 degrees. In a bowl, cut the flour into the shortening. Add buttermilk a little at a time. Knead the dough, but not too much. Pull off a piece of dough the size of a golf ball and dip wet end into flour and roll into a ball, then flatten and smooth with thumb. Place the biscuits on a greased cookie sheet. Dab buttermilk on top of each biscuit. Bake at 450 degrees for 8 to 10 minutes until the biscuits are golden brown.

Yields: 48 biscuits

Louise Rush

♦ ANGEL BISCUITS ♦

1	package activated dry yeast
2 to 3	tablespoons warm water
5	cups all-purpose flour
3 to 5	tablespoons sugar
1	tablespoon baking powder
1	teaspoon salt
1	cup vegetable shortening
1	teaspoon baking soda
2	cups buttermilk

Preheat oven to 400 degrees. Dissolve the yeast in the warm water.

Sift the flour, sugar, salt, baking powder and baking soda together. Cut the shortening into the flour mixture. Stir in the yeast mixture and buttermilk. Roll out on floured board and cut out with biscuit cutter. Brush tops of biscuits with melted butter. Bake at 400 degrees for 10 to 20 minutes, or until golden brown.

This dough will keep refrigerated for several days; allow the refrigerated dough to rise before baking.

Yields: 48 biscuits

Eleanor Helms

◆ Bojangles Biscuits ◆

2	cups self-rising flour
2	teaspoons baking powder
2	teaspoons confectioners' sugar
1/3	cup vegetable shortening
3/4 to 1	cup buttermilk

Preheat oven to 450 degrees. Mix all ingredients together. Roll dough to 1/2-inch thickness and cut with a 2-inch biscuit cutter. Bake biscuits on a lightly greased baking sheet at 450 degrees for 10 to 12 minutes or until biscuits are lightly browned.

Yields: 36 biscuits

Pat Rush

◆ Easy Herb Biscuits ◆

2	cups biscuit mix
1	tablespoon freeze-dried chives
1	teaspoon dried parsley flakes
3/4	cup plain yogurt

Preheat oven to 450 degrees. Combine all ingredients in a medium bowl, stirring until dry ingredients are moistened. Turn dough out onto a floured surface, and knead lightly four or five times.

Roll dough to 1/2-inch thickness and cut with a 2-inch biscuit cutter. Place biscuits on a lightly greased baking sheet. Bake at 450 degrees for eight minutes or until biscuits are lightly browned.

Yields: 12 biscuits

Karen Harris

◆ COUNTRY WHEAT ◆
DROP BISCUITS

1	cup buttermilk, heated to lukewarm
1	cup shredded wheat squares
1	package active dry yeast
1/4	cup warm water
2	cups all-purpose flour
4	tablespoons sugar
1	teaspoon baking powder
1/2	teaspoon baking soda
1/2	teaspoon salt
1/3	cup vegetable shortening

Preheat oven to 375 degrees. Pour the buttermilk over the cereal and set aside.

Combine the flour, sugar, baking powder, baking soda and salt. Cut in the shortening until it resembles course meal. Add the cereal mixture and the yeast to the flour mixture, stirring until moistened. Drop dough by heaping tablespoons about 2-inches apart on lightly greased baking sheet. Bake at 375 degrees for 15 to 18 minutes.

Yields: 18 biscuits

Margaret Young

◆ CURRANT SCONES ◆

A great brunch or breakfast bread to serve guests!

2	*cups all-purpose flour*
2	*tablespoons sugar*
2	*teaspoons baking powder*
1/2	*teaspoon salt*
3/4	*cup margarine or butter*
1 1/2	*cups currants*
1/3 to 1/2	*cup milk*

Preheat oven to 450 degrees. Combine the flour, sugar, baking powder, and salt. Cut in the margarine with a pastry blender until the mixture resembles course meal. Stir in currants. Gradually add enough milk to the mixture to form a soft dough, stirring just until dry ingredients are moistened. Turn dough out onto a lightly floured surface, and knead lightly four or five times.

Roll dough to 1/2-inch thickness and cut with a 2-inch biscuit cutter. Bake on a lightly greased baking sheets at 450 degrees for 8 to 10 minutes or until lightly browned. Serve warm.

Yields: 24 scones

Karen Harris

◆ CHEDDAR MUFFINS ◆

2	cups all-purpose flour, unsifted
1	tablespoon baking powder
1	teaspoon sugar
1/2	teaspoon salt
1	cup milk
4	tablespoons (1/2 stick) margarine or butter, melted
1	large egg
1	cup coarsely shredded cheddar cheese
2	teaspoons chopped fresh chives

Preheat oven to 400 degrees. Grease 24 muffin-pan cups. In a large bowl, combine the flour, baking powder, sugar, and salt.

In a small bowl, combine the milk, margarine, and egg. Stir the milk mixture into the flour mixture until the flour is moistened. (Batter will be lumpy). Fold in the cheese and chives. Using a small spoon, divide the batter among greased muffin-pan cups.

Bake at 400 degrees for 10 to 12 minutes, or until centers spring back when lightly pressed with fingertip. Cool muffins in pan on wire rack for 5 minutes. Remove muffins from pan and serve warm.

Yields: 24 muffins

Margaret Young

♦ Jalapeno ♦
Corn Muffins

1 1/4	cups all-purpose flour, unsifted
3/4	cup yellow corn flour
1	tablespoon baking powder
1	teaspoon sugar
1/2	teaspoon salt
1	cup milk
4	tablespoons (1/2 stick) margarine or butter, melted
1	large egg
1	small red jalapeno pepper, chopped with stem, ribs and seeds removed
1	cup fresh or frozen corn
1	tablespoon chopped cilantro

Preheat oven to 400 degrees. Grease 24 muffin-pan cups. In a large bowl, combine the flours, baking powder, sugar, and salt.

In a small bowl, combine the milk, margarine, and egg. Stir the milk mixture into the flour mixture until the flour is moistened. (Batter will be lumpy). Fold in the pepper, corn and cilantro. Using a small spoon, divide the batter among greased muffin-pan cups.

Bake at 400 degrees for 10 to 12 minutes, or until centers spring back when lightly pressed with fingertip. Serve immediately.

Yields: 24 muffins

Margaret Young

♦ COMPANY MUFFINS ♦

1	cup all-purpose flour
1	cup oat bran
2	teaspoons baking soda
1	teaspoon baking powder
1/2	teaspoon salt
2	teaspoons cinnamon
1	cup brown sugar
1	cup drained pineapple
2	large tart apples, peeled, cored and shredded
1/2	cup raisins, optional
1	cup chopped pecans
1/4	cup vegetable oil
1/2	cup skim milk
2	eggs, slightly beaten
1	teaspoon vanilla

Preheat oven to 375 degrees. Combine the flour, oat bran, baking soda, baking powder, salt and cinnamon in a large bowl. Stir in the sugar. Add the pineapple, apples, raisins and nuts. Stir well.

Make a well in the center of the flour mixture. Add the oil, milk, eggs and vanilla. Stir flour mixture until just moistened. Use a 1/4 cup measure to scoop muffin batter into greased muffin tins. Bake at 375 degrees for 18 to 20 minutes, or until nicely browned.

Yields: 18 muffins

Bob Rush

♦ APPLE MUFFINS ♦

3 1/2	cups all-purpose flour
3	cups finely chopped apples
2	cups sugar
1	teaspoon salt
1	teaspoon baking soda
1	teaspoon cinnamon
1	teaspoon vanilla flavoring
1 1/2	cups vegetable oil
1/2 to 3/4	cups chopped pecans

Preheat oven to 350 degrees. Combine the flour, apples, sugar, salt, baking soda and cinnamon in a large bowl. Stir in the oil, nuts, and vanilla. Batter will be stiff.

Fill muffin cups 1/2 to 2/3 full. Bake at 350 degrees for about 30 minutes, until toothpick comes out clean.

Yields: 24 muffins

Kathy Eudy

♦ PINEAPPLE MUFFINS ♦

2	cups all-purpose flour
2 1/2	teaspoons baking powder
1/2	teaspoon baking soda
1/2	teaspoon salt
1/2	cup firmly packed brown sugar
1/3	cup vegetable oil
1	egg
1	cup sour cream
1	8-ounce can crushed pineapple, undrained

Preheat oven to 350 degrees. Sift the flour, baking powder, baking soda, and salt together. In a large bowl, combine the dry ingredients with the brown sugar. In a separate bowl, mix the egg, sour cream, pineapple and oil. Add liquid ingredients to the dry ingredients, mixing only until moistened. Spoon into paper-lined muffin cups, filling 2/3 full. Bake at 350 degrees for 25 minutes, or until brown.

Yields: 14 to 16 muffins

Deborah Alston

♦Raisin Bran Muffins♦

1	15-ounce box Raisin Bran cereal
2 1/2	cups sugar
5	cups all-purpose flour
5	teaspoons baking soda
2	teaspoons salt
1	cup oil
4	eggs, beaten
1	quart buttermilk

Preheat oven to 400 degrees. Mix the cereal, sugar, flour, baking soda and salt in a large bowl. Add the oil, eggs, and buttermilk to the dry mixture. Mix well.

Fill muffin tins 2/3 full. Bake at 400 degrees for 18 to 20 minutes. Dough may be refrigerated in a covered bowl for up to six weeks.

Yields: 36 muffins

Jackie Brown

♦ OAT-NUT ♦
BRAN MUFFINS

5	cups all-purpose flour, sifted
2	cups sugar
5	teaspoons baking soda
1	teaspoon salt
4	teaspoons cinnamon
1	cup All-Bran cereal
1	cup oatmeal
1	cup Oat Bran cereal
2	cups 40% Bran Flakes
2	cups raisins
2	cups chopped pecans
1	cup Puritan Oil
4	eggs or one 8-ounce carton Egg Beaters
1	cup water
1	cup apple sauce
1	quart buttermilk

Preheat oven to 400 degrees. Sift the flour, sugar, baking soda, salt and cinnamon together. Add the cereals, raisins, and nuts to the flour mixture.

In a bowl, combine the milk, eggs, oil, water and apple sauce. Stir liquid mixture with dry mixture only until moist. Fill greased muffin tins 2/3 full. Bake at 400 degrees for 20 minutes. Dough may be refrigerated in a covered bowl for four to six weeks.

Yields: 48 muffins

Jackie Brown

◆ EASY BANANA BREAD ◆

1	cup sugar
1	8-ounce package cream cheese
2	ripe, medium bananas, mashed
2	eggs
2	cups Bisquick
1/2	cup nuts

Preheat oven to 350 degrees. Mix the sugar, cream cheese, bananas, eggs and Bisquick. Fold in the nuts. Bake at 350 degrees for one hour. The baked bread refrigerates and freezes well.

Yields: 1 loaf

Eleanor Helms

◆ NUTTY BANANA ◆
BREAD

1 1/2	cups all-purpose flour
1	teaspoon baking soda
1/2	teaspoon salt
1	egg, slightly beaten
1	cup sugar
4	tablespoons margarine or butter, melted
3	ripe medium bananas, mashed
1	cup chopped nuts, optional

Preheat oven to 325 degrees. Combine the flour, baking soda and salt in a medium bowl. In a small bowl, mix the egg, sugar and margarine. Add the bananas to the sugar mixture. Combine the sugar mixture with the flour mixture. Add the nuts, if desired.

Pour into a greased 6-cup loaf pan. Bake at 325 degrees for 60 to 75 minutes. Batter may be used to make muffins. Fill muffin tins 2/3 full. Bake at 350 degrees for 25 to 30 minutes.

Yields: 1 loaf or 12 muffins

Deborah Alston

◆ BANANA NUT BREAD ◆

2   sticks margarine
2   cups sugar
4   eggs
6   bananas, mashed
4   cups all-purpose flour
2   teaspoons baking powder
2   cups chopped nuts
2   cups raisins

Preheat oven to 325 degrees. Mix the margarine, sugar, eggs, bananas, flour and baking powder. Fold in the chopped nuts and raisins. Pour the mixture into two large, greased pans. Bake at 325 degrees for one hour.

Yields: 2 large loaves

Pat Rush

♦ CRANBERRY BREAD ♦

1   cup sugar
2   cups self-rising flour
1/4   cup vegetable shortening
3/4   cup orange juice
1   tablespoon grated orange rind
1   egg, well beaten
1/2   cup chopped English walnuts
2   cups chopped fresh cranberries

Preheat oven to 350 degrees. Sift the sugar and flour. Cut the shortening into the flour until the mixture resembles coarse cornmeal. In a small bowl, combine the orange juice, rind and egg. Pour the juice mixture into the dry ingredients, mixing just enough to dampen. Fold in the cranberries and nuts.

Spoon the dough into 9x5-inch greased loaf pan. Bake at 350 degrees for about one hour. Remove from pan and cool. Wrap well for storing. This bread also freezes nicely.

Yields: 1 loaf

Margaret Young

◆ CORNBREAD ◆

1	cup all-purpose flour
1	cup white corn meal
1/2	teaspoon salt
4	teaspoons baking powder
1/4	cup sugar
2	eggs
1	cup milk
1	tablespoon vegetable oil

Preheat oven to 375 degrees. Mix the flour, meal, salt, baking powder and sugar. Combine the eggs, milk and oil. Add the egg mixture to the dry ingredients and stir. Pour the batter into greased iron skillet and bake at 375 degrees for 25 minutes. For a "crustier" cornbread, preheat the greased pan in the oven.

Margaret Young

◆ RICH BUT DELISH ◆ CORNBREAD

1/2	stick margarine or butter
1	cup self-rising yellow corn meal (not corn meal mix)
2	eggs
1	cup cream style corn
1	cup sour cream
1/2	small onion, grated

Preheat oven to 375 degrees. In a 9-inch skillet, melt margarine in the oven until it bubbles. While margarine is melting, mix together the corn meal, eggs, corn, sour cream and onion. Pour mixture into skillet on top of margarine. Be careful not to let the butter scorch. Bake at 375 degrees for 40 minutes.

Gwen Allen

◆ GWEN'S CORNBREAD ◆

1	cup self-rising yellow corn meal (not a corn meal mix)
1	cup self-rising flour
1	cup milk
2	eggs
1/4	cup corn oil
1/4	cup sugar

Preheat oven to 400 degrees. In a mixer, pour the milk, eggs and oil and mix. Add the corn meal, flour and sugar. Mix while scraping sides of container with rubber spatula until mixed. (Do not over beat). Pour into a well greased square or round cake pan. Bake at 400 degrees for 30 minutes.

Gwen Allen

♦ TURKEY DRESSING ♦

Gwen had never measured her ingredients for
Turkey Dressing, until we asked for her recipe.
This dressing is wonderful!

	Gwen's cornbread (page 96), cooled
1/4	box saltine crackers, crushed
3	hard boiled eggs, chopped course
1 1/2	cup celery, chopped very fine
1	cup onion, chopped very fine
2	tablespoon sage
2	tablespoons poultry seasoning
2	tablespoons sugar
1	cup broth from turkey
1	cup canned chicken broth

Preheat oven to 425 degrees. In a large bowl, break up the cornbread fine. Pour the crushed crackers on top of cornbread. Add the eggs, celery, onion, sage, seasoning, and sugar. Mix well.

Pour the broth over dry ingredients, stirring until the mixture is well moistened but not too wet. Taste the mixture and add additional sage and poultry seasoning, as desired.

Pour mixture into a greased 9x12-inch pyrex dish. Bake at 425 degrees for approximately 30 minutes or until slightly brown on top.

Yields: 12 to 15 servings

Gwen Allen

◆ CORN SPOON BREAD ◆

2	cups hot milk
1/3	cup corn meal
3	tablespoons butter
3	tablespoons fresh bread crumbs
3	ears corn, cut and scraped
1	green onion, chopped
2	egg yolks, at room temperature
2	egg whites, at room temperature
2	teaspoons sugar
	Salt and pepper to taste

Preheat oven to 325 degrees. Combine the cornmeal and milk. Over medium-high heat, stir the mixture and cook until thickened. Remove from heat. Add the butter, bread crumbs, corn, and onion to the cornmeal mixture.

Beat the egg yolks at medium speed with an electric mixer until thick and lemon colored. Stir yolks into cornmeal mixture. Beat egg whites until stiff but not dry. Gently fold into cornmeal mixture.

Pour into a lightly greased casserole dish. Bake at 325 degrees for 1 to 1 1/4 hours, until a knife inserted in center comes out clean.

Yields: 6 to 8 servings

Margaret Young

♦ BLUEBERRY ♦
COFFEE CAKE

1/2	cup margarine or butter
1	cup sugar
2	eggs
2	cups all-purpose flour
1	teaspoon baking soda
1	teaspoon baking powder
1/2	teaspoon salt
1	cup sour cream
1	teaspoon vanilla
1	can drained blueberries (approximately 2 cups)
1/3	cup brown sugar
1/4	cup sugar
1	teaspoon cinnamon

Preheat the oven to 325 degrees. Cream the margarine. Add the sugar and cream until fluffy. Add the eggs, beating well after each. Sift the flour, baking soda, baking powder, and salt. Add the dry mixture to the butter mixture, reserving approximately 1/4 cup of the dry mixture to coat the blueberries. Pour the reserved dry mixture on the blueberries and toss lightly. Add the sour cream and blueberries to mixture by hand. Stir in the vanilla.

Mix the brown sugar, sugar, and cinnamon. Pour 1/2 the batter into a greased bundt pan. Sprinkle 1/2 sugar mixture; add rest of batter, then sprinkle the remaining sugar. Bake at 325 degrees for 40 minutes.

Yields: 8 servings

Deborah Alston

◆ COUNTRY APPLE ◆
COFFEE CAKE

2	tablespoons margarine or butter, softened
1 1/2	cups peeled, chopped apples
1	10-ounce can Hungry Jack Flaky, Buttermilk Flaky, or Butter Tastin' Flaky Biscuits
1/3	cup firmly packed brown sugar
1/4	teaspoon cinnamon
1/3	cup light corn syrup
1 1/2	teaspoons whiskey, if desired
1	egg
1/2	cup pecan halves or pieces
1/3	cup powdered sugar
1/4	teaspoon vanilla
1-2	teaspoons milk

Heat oven to 350 degrees. Using one tablespoon of margarine, generously grease bottom and sides of 9-inch round cake pan or 8-inch square pan. Spread one cup of the apples in the prepared pan. Separate dough into 10 biscuits. Cut each into four pieces. Arrange biscuit pieces point-side-up over apples. Top with remaining apples. In a small bowl, combine the remaining margarine, brown sugar, cinnamon, corn syrup, whiskey and egg. Beat for two to three minutes until sugar is partially dissolved. Stir in the pecans and spoon over biscuit pieces.

Bake at 350 degrees for 35 to 45 minutes or until deep golden brown. Cool for five minutes. Blend the powdered sugar, vanilla, and milk until smooth. Drizzle the glaze over the warm coffee cake.

Yields: **8 servings**

Margaret Young

◆Cinnamon Roll Ring◆

1	package active dry yeast
3/4	cup warm water
1	package hot-roll mix
1	egg, unbeaten
1/4	cup honey
2	tablespoons margarine or butter
2	tablespoons honey
1/2	cup brown sugar, firmly packed
1	teaspoon cinnamon
3/4	cup raisins
1/2	cup chopped nuts
1	cup powdered confectioners' sugar
2-3	tablespoons milk

Sprinkle the yeast over warm (not hot) water in large mixing bowl; stir to dissolve. Add the egg, honey, and hot-roll dry mix; blend well. Let the dough rise in warm place, away from draft, about one hour, until light and doubled in bulk.

Roll dough out on lightly floured board into a 20x12-inch rectangle. Combine the margarine and honey and spread evenly on dough. Combine the brown sugar, cinnamon, raisins, and nuts and sprinkle over the dough. Roll as a jelly roll from wide side; cut into 16 slices. Arrange the slices, with the flat side down, in a two layers in well-greased 10-inch tube pan. Cover and let rise in warm place, away from draft, for one hour, or until doubled in bulk. Preheat oven to 350 degrees.

Bake at 350 degrees for 40 for 45 minutes, or until browned. Blend the powdered sugar and milk. Frost the rolls while still warm.

Yields: 36 rolls

Margaret Young

◆ RAISIN-CINNAMON ◆
ROLLS

1	16-ounce loaf frozen bread dough, thawed
4	tablespoons margarine or butter, divided and melted
1/2	cup sugar
2	teaspoons ground cinnamon
1/3	cup raisins
2	tablespoons chopped almonds, toasted
2	teaspoons grated lemon rind
1/2	cup sifted powdered sugar
2 1/2	teaspoons lemon juice

Roll dough on a lightly floured surface into a 14x8-inch rectangle. Brush surface with two tablespoons margarine.

Combine the sugar, cinnamon, raisins, almonds, and lemon rind. Sprinkle over dough, leaving a 1/2-inch border on all sides. Starting with long side, roll up jelly roll fashion. Pinch seam to seal, but do not seal the ends.

Cut the roll into 12 slices. Place in a lightly greased 9-inch square pan. Brush with the remaining margarine. Cover and refrigerate 8 hours.

Remove the dough from the refrigerator, and let rise in a warm place (85 degrees) free from drafts, for 50 minutes or until doubled in bulk. Bake at 350 degrees for 20 to 25 minutes.

Combine the powdered sugar and lemon juice. Drizzle the icing over warm rolls.

Yields: 24 rolls

Margaret Young

◆ BEEF AND PORK ◆

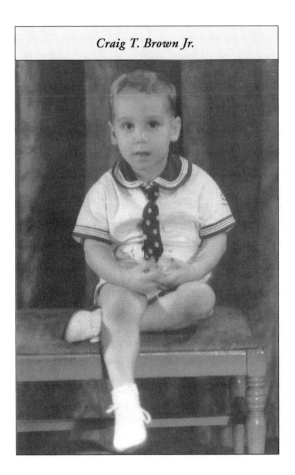

Craig T. Brown Jr.

This cute fella later joined the family as Jackie's husband.

Granny's life was blessed with a wonderful daughter-in-law and four terrific sons-in-law. No one remembers ever hearing Granny utter a word of criticism about any of her children's spouses.

Craig Brown was one of the Granny's treasures. I first met Craig when he was dating Jackie. As a toddler, I was outside on the front stoop with Jackie "helping" her sweep the walk. As children do, I got in the way of her broom and was whacked in the head, just as Craig approached to pick Jackie up for a date. To her horror, Craig swept me up in his arms, soothed my hurt feelings and chastised Jackie. I have loved Craig ever since. Craig forgave Jackie and married her in 1959.

◆ SWEET & SOUR ◆
BEEF STEW

1 1/2	pounds beef, cut into 1-inch cubes
2	tablespoons oil
1	cup chopped carrots
1	cup sliced onions
1	8-ounce can tomato sauce
1/4	cup brown sugar
1/4	cup vinegar
1	tablespoon Worcestershire sauce
1	teaspoon salt
1 1/4	cups water, divided
4	teaspoons cornstarch

In a heavy 4-quart saucepan, brown the beef in the oil. Drain and add carrots, onions, tomato sauce, sugar, vinegar, and Worcestershire sauce. Cook covered over low heat for two hours.

As the stew cooks, add one cup water and the salt a little at a time. In a small bowl, combine the cornstarch and 1/4 cup water and stir. After beef stew cooks, add the cornstarch mixture. Simmer an additional 30 minutes.

Yields: 6 servings

Deborah Alston

♦ A LA JONES ♦
BEEF STEW

2	tablespoons vegetable shortening
1	tablespoon sugar
1/4	cup all-purpose flour
2	pounds beef, cut into 1-inch cubes
1	teaspoon chili powder
1/4	teaspoon thyme
1	bay leaf
1	beef bouillon cube
1	cup water
2 to 3	peeled and quartered ripe fresh tomatoes
6	potatoes, peeled and cubed
6	carrots, peeled and sliced
1	large onion, chopped
6	celery stalks, chopped
2	10-ounce packages of frozen vegetables, such as peas, limas, or corn

Heat the shortening in a large pan. Combine the sugar and flour; coat the beef in the flour mixture and cook the beef in hot shortening. Add the chili powder, thyme, bay leaf, bouillon cube and water. Cover and simmer for 15 minutes. Add the tomatoes, potatoes, carrots, onions, celery and frozen vegetables and simmer on low heat for 1 1/2 to 2 hours.

Yields: 6 servings

Debbie Brown

◆ OVEN BEEF STEW ◆

3	pounds stew beef, cut into 1-inch cubes
3/4	cup carrots, peeled and sliced
2	stalks celery, sliced
2	onions, sliced
2	teaspoons sugar
3 to 4	potatoes, peeled and cubed
2	tablespoons tapioca
1 1/2	cups tomato juice

Preheat oven to 250 degrees. Combine the beef, carrots, celery, onions, sugar, potatoes, tapioca and tomato juice. Place the beef mixture in a covered, greased casserole and bake at 250 degrees for four hours.

Yields: 6 to 8 servings

Margaret Young

♦ ITALIAN BEEF ♦
STIR FRY

1	pound beef round tip steaks, cut 1/8 to 1/4-inch thick
2	cloves garlic, crushed
1	tablespoon olive oil
2	small zucchini, thinly sliced
1	cup cherry tomato halves
1/4	cup bottled Italian salad dressing
2	cups hot cooked spaghetti
1	tablespoon grated Parmesan cheese

Cut the beef steaks crosswise into 1-inch wide strips. Cut each strip crosswise in half. Stir the garlic in oil in a large non-stick skillet and cook over medium-high heat for one minute. Add the beef strips (1/2 at a time) and stir-fry for 1 to 1 1/2 minutes. Season with salt and pepper. Remove with slotted spoon. Keep warm.

Add the zucchini and stir-fry 2 to 3 minutes or until crisp-tender. Return beef to skillet with tomato halves and salad dressing and heat through. Serve over hot pasta. Garnish with cheese.

Yields: 4 servings

Deborah Alston

◆ SWISS STEAK ◆

Tender and flavorful.

6	6-ounce cubed steaks
1/4	cup all-purpose flour
	Salt and pepper to taste
3	tablespoons peanut, vegetable or corn oil
1	cup coarsely chopped onion
1	clove garlic, finely minced
1/2	cup dry white wine
2	cups water
1/2	teaspoon dried thyme
1	bay leaf
1	cup chopped celery
1	tablespoon tomato paste
4	large carrots, peeled and quartered (about 1/2-pound)
1	cup frozen peas

If desired, pound the steak lightly. Dredge both sides of the steaks with flour, seasoned with salt and pepper, immediately before browning.

Heat the oil in a deep, heavy skillet and brown the steaks for about five minutes on each side. Pour off the fat from the skillet. Add the onion and garlic and cook briefly. Add the wine, water, thyme, bay leaf and celery. Stir in the tomato paste. Cover and cook over medium-low heat for about one hour. Add the carrots and cook for 40 minutes longer, or until meat is fork-tender. Add the peas and cook for another five minutes.

Yields: 6 servings

Karen Harris

♦ GRANNY'S ♦
ROAST BEEF

An old family favorite.

Beef:

1	bottom round, rump or sirloin tip roast
1 to 2	tablespoons vegetable oil
	Water

Gravy:

1	cup water
2	tablespoons all-purpose flour
	Salt and pepper to taste

To prepare the beef: On medium-high heat, brown the fat side of the beef in oil first, then brown the remaining sides of the beef. After the meat is well browned, add approximately 2-inches of water to the pan. Cook on medium-low heat for two to three hours. Check periodically to be sure that water is in the pan. Turn the heat up to high, and sear the meat on all sides again. Remove the meat from the pan.

To prepare the gravy: In a small bowl, combine the water and flour and mix well. Pour the flour mixture through a strainer, into the beef juices. Add salt and pepper to taste.

Place the meat in the gravy and return to low heat until ready to serve.

Yields: weight of beef will determine number of servings

Gladys Allen

◆ Sirloin Tip Roast ◆

1   sirloin tip roast

Preheat oven to 500 degrees. Place the roast in a large pan, uncovered. Cook at 500 degrees for five minutes per pound of beef. Cut the oven off; leave the pan in the oven for two hours.

Yields: weight of beef will determine number of servings

Jackie Brown

◆ Beef Tenderloin ◆

7   pounds with fat, or 5 pounds trimmed fat tenderloin,
         trimmed very well and membrane film removed
         Water
         Garlic salt
         Seasoned salt

Preheat oven to 450 degrees. Place the meat on a broiler rack in a pan with a small amount of water in the bottom. Season with garlic salt and seasoned salt. Bake at 450 degrees for seven minutes. Reduce heat to 350 degrees for 30 to 40 minutes.

Yields: 8 servings

Eleanor Helms

✦ LASAGNA ✦

Meat Sauce:

2	*tablespoons vegetable oil*
1/2	*cup chopped onion*
1	*clove garlic, crushed*
2	*tablespoons chopped parsley*
3	*pounds lean ground beef*
2	*28-ounce cans tomatoes*
1	*6-ounce can tomato paste*
1	*can tomato sauce*
2	*tablespoons sugar*
1	*tablespoon salt*
2	*teaspoons oregano leaves*
1	*teaspoon basil leaves*
1/4	*teaspoon pepper*
1	*pound cottage cheese*
1	*pound Mozzarella cheese, thinly sliced*
3	*ounces grated Parmesan cheese*

Noodles:

1	*tablespoon salt*
1	*tablespoon oil*
1	*pound lasagna noodles*

To make meat sauce: In two tablespoons oil, saute the onion, garlic and parsley for five minutes. Add the beef and brown. Add tomatoes, tomato paste, tomato sauce, sugar, salt, oregano, basil, and pepper. Bring to boil and simmer for one hour.

To cook noodles: Bring to a boil three quarts water, salt and oil in a large pot. Add noodles two to three at the time. Boil for 15 minutes. Drain and rinse with hot water.

Preheat oven to 350 degrees. Grease two large flat baking dishes. Spoon a little tomato sauce into the prepared pans. Layer noodles, cottage cheese, mozzarella, meat sauce and Parmesan. Repeat until all is used, ending with sauce and Parmesan. Bake at 350 degrees uncovered for 45 minutes. Let stand 15 minutes to make serving easier. Freezes beautifully.

Yields: 12 servings

Jackie Brown

◆ ELAINE'S ◆
MEXICAN LASAGNA

1	pound hamburger
1	cup chopped onions
1	package chili seasoning mix
2	8-ounce cans tomato sauce
1	15-ounce can Ranch Style beans
1/2 to 3/4	cup water
1	package flour tortillas
1/2	pound cheddar cheese
1	small package Mozzarella cheese

Preheat oven to 350 degrees. Brown the hamburger and onion in a medium sauce pan. Drain the grease. Add the chili seasoning, tomato sauce, beans, water. Simmer for ten minutes. Cut the flour tortillas in small squares.

In a 9x13-inch dish arrange in layers the tortillas, chili mix, both cheeses, ending with cheeses. Bake at 350 degrees about 30 minutes, until the cheese melts.

Yields: 6 to 8 servings

Deborah Alston

◆ BARBECUED ◆ MEATBALLS

1	cup soft bread crumbs
1/2	cup milk
1	pound ground beef
1	teaspoon salt
1	teaspoon pepper
1 1/2	tablespoons Worcestershire sauce
1/4	cup vinegar
1	tablespoon sugar
1/2	cup ketchup
1/2	cup water
1/2	cup chopped green pepper
1/2	cup chopped onion

Preheat the oven to 375 degrees. Moisten the bread crumbs with milk, combine with the ground beef, salt and pepper. Shape mixture into balls. Place in 9-inch baking dish.

Combine the Worcestershire sauce, vinegar, sugar, ketchup, water, green pepper and onion. Pour around meatballs. Bake uncovered at 375 degrees for 45 minutes.

Yields: 8 servings

Deborah Alston

♦ CHEESEBURGER PIE ♦

1	pound ground beef
1/2	cup evaporated milk
1/2	cup ketchup
1/3	cup dry bread crumbs
2	tablespoons dried leaf oregano
3/4	teaspoon salt
1/2	teaspoon pepper
1	deep dish pie shell, unbaked
4	ounces American or mild cheddar cheese, grated
1	teaspoon Worcestershire sauce

Preheat oven to 350 degrees. Combine the ground beef, milk, ketchup, bread crumbs, oregano, salt and pepper in a large bowl. Mix well with hands. Pat mixture into the pie shell.

Bake at 350 degrees for 30 to 35 minutes. Toss cheese with Worcestershire sauce and sprinkle on top of pie. Bake ten minutes longer. Cool 10 minutes. Baked pie may be frozen.

Yields: 6 servings

Karen Harris

◆ PIZZA BURGERS ◆

1   *pound lean ground beef*
1   *15-ounce can pizza sauce*
1   *teaspoon dried oregano*
1/2   *medium onion, diced*
1/2   *medium green pepper, sliced*
6   *hamburger buns, split*
1/2   *cup shredded mozzarella cheese*

In a skillet, brown the ground beef and drain. Stir in the pizza sauce and oregano. Add the onion and pepper to beef mixture. Simmer for 20 to 25 minutes. Spoon mixture on top of buns. Top with cheese and serve immediately.

Yields: 6 servings

Pat Rush

♦ MEAT LOAF ♦

Meat Loaf:

1	pound ground beef
1	cup bread crumbs
1/2	medium onion, chopped
1/2	8-ounce can tomato sauce
1	egg, beaten
1/2	teaspoon salt
1/4	teaspoon pepper
1/4	green pepper, chopped

Sweet and Sour Sauce:

2	tablespoons prepared mustard
2	tablespoons brown sugar
1/2	8-ounce can tomato sauce
1/2	cup water
2	tablespoons vinegar

To prepare the meat loaf: Preheat the oven to 350 degrees. Combine the ground beef, bread crumbs, onion, tomato sauce, egg, salt, pepper and green pepper in a large bowl. Mix well with hands. Pat mixture into a loaf pan.

To prepare the sauce: Combine the mustard, brown sugar, tomato sauce, water and vinegar.

Baste the meat loaf with the sauce. Bake at 350 degrees for one hour. Baste the meat loaf several times with the sauce while baking.

Yields: 4 to 6 servings

Jackie Brown

♦ BLENDER MEAT LOAF ♦

2	slices fresh bread, crumbled
2	pounds ground lean beef
1/2	pound ground lean pork
2	eggs
1/2	cup tomato juice or V-8 juice
1	medium onion
2	teaspoons salt
1/2	teaspoon pepper
1	tablespoon Worcestershire sauce

Preheat oven to 350 degrees. Mix the crumbs, beef and pork. In a blender, combine the eggs, tomato juice, onion, salt, pepper and Worcestershire sauce and pulse. Combine the liquid mixture with the meat. Pat the mixture into a loaf pan. Bake at 350 degrees for one hour.

Yields: 8 servings

Margaret Young

♦ HUNT'S QUICK ♦
SPAGHETTI SAUCE

1	pound ground beef
2	16-ounce cans tomato sauce
1/2	cup water
1	2-ounce can sliced mushrooms, drained
2	tablespoons minced onion flakes
1 1/2	teaspoons brown sugar, packed
3/4	teaspoon oregano
1/2	teaspoon basil
1/2	teaspoon garlic salt
1/8	teaspoon marjoram
12	ounces spaghetti, cooked and drained
	Parmesan cheese, optional

In a large frying pan with cover, brown the ground beef and drain the fat. Add the tomato sauce, water, mushrooms, onion flakes, brown sugar, oregano, basil, garlic salt and marjoram. Cook covered on medium-low heat for 1 to 1 1/2 hours. Serve sauce over cooked spaghetti and garnish with Parmesan cheese.

Yields: 6 to 8 servings

Martha Helms

♦ SPAGHETTI WITH ♦ ITALIAN MEAT SAUCE

A family favorite.

1	cup chopped onion
1 1/2	pounds ground chuck or ground round, browned
2	cloves garlic, crushed
2	28-ounce cans tomatoes, crushed
1	6-ounce can tomato paste
6	ounces water, optional
2	stalks celery, capped and chopped
2	teaspoons salt
1/2	teaspoon M.S.G.
3	teaspoons dried oregano
1/4	teaspoons dried thyme
1	bay leaf
1	16-ounce box and one 4-ounce box Vermicelli spaghetti, cooked and drained

In a crock pot, combine all ingredients and stir thoroughly. Cover and cook on high for one hour. Reduce to low heat and cook for 10 hours.

Yields: 10 to 12 servings

Eleanor Helms

◆ CHILI ◆

2	*16-ounce cans kidney beans, drained*
2	*16-ounce cans tomatoes, chopped up*
2	*pounds ground chuck, browned and drained*
2	*medium onions, chopped*
1	*green pepper, chopped*
2	*cloves garlic, crushed*
2	*tablespoons chili powder*
1	*teaspoon pepper*
1	*teaspoon cumin*
	Salt to taste

In a crock pot, combine the kidney beans, tomatoes, beef, onions, pepper, garlic, chili powder, pepper, cumin and salt and stir once. Cover and cook on high for 1 hour. Reduce heat setting to low and cook for 10 to 12 hours.

Yields: 8 to 10 servings

Eleanor Helms

◆ That's Chili ◆

1	*pound lean ground beef*
1	*clove garlic, minced (about 1 teaspoon)*
1	*large onion, finely chopped (about 1 cup)*
1	*medium green pepper, finely chopped (about 2/3 cup)*
1	*tablespoon chili powder*
1	*tablespoon cider vinegar*
1/4	*teaspoon allspice*
1/4	*teaspoon coriander*
1	*teaspoon cumin*
1/2	*teaspoon salt, or to taste*
1/2	*cup water*
1	*16-ounce can crushed tomatoes*
1	*16-ounce can red kidney beans, with liquid*
1	*4-ounce can green chilies, chopped (optional)*

Cook the beef, garlic, onion, and green pepper in a heavy skillet over medium-high heat, stirring frequently to break up meat. Cook until onion is soft and meat has lost its pink color. Add the chili powder, vinegar, allspice, coriander, cumin, salt, water, tomatoes and kidney beans. Bring to a boil. Cover and reduce heat. Simmer the chili for 45 minutes, stirring frequently.

Yields: 8 servings

Sam Harris

◆ SAUSAGE CASSEROLE ◆

1	pound sausage, browned and drained
8	eggs, beaten
1	teaspoon salt
1	cup sharp cheese, grated
1	teaspoon prepared mustard
2	cups milk
2	slices of bread, cubed

Preheat the oven to 350 degrees. Combine the sausage, eggs, salt, cheese, mustard, and milk. Place the bread cubes in the bottom of a casserole dish. Pour the sausage mixture over the bread.

Bake at 350 degrees for 40 to 45 minutes.

Yields: 8 servings

Eleanor Helms

♦ HAM LOAF ♦

A great dish to serve company!

Ham loaf:
1	pound ground ham
1	pound lean sausage, at room temperature
2	cups soft bread crumbs
2	eggs
1	cup sour cream
1/3	cup chopped onion
2	tablespoons lemon juice
1	teaspoon curry powder
1	teaspoon ground ginger
1	teaspoon powdered mustard
1/8	teaspoon grated nutmeg
1/8	teaspoon paprika

Basting sauce:
1	cup brown sugar
1/2	cup water
1/2	cup cider vinegar
1/4	teaspoon black pepper

Preheat oven to 350 degrees.

To prepare the ham loaf: Combine the ham, sausage and bread crumbs in a large mixer bowl, using your hands if necessary. In a medium bowl, beat the eggs and add the sour cream, onion, lemon juice, and spices. Mix well, pour over the meat mixture, and blend. Form mixture into a loaf and place in an oiled 9x13-inch baking dish. Bake uncovered at 350 degrees for 1 hour.

To prepare the basting sauce: Combine the brown sugar, water, vinegar, and pepper in a small saucepan and bring to a boil.

When the ham loaf has baked for 40 minutes, remove from oven and drain off any excess fat. Pour the sauce over the loaf and continue baking another 15 minutes, basting occasionally with the pan juices.

Yields: 8 servings

Karen Harris

♦ EASY GRILLED HAM ♦

1   2" *fully cooked ham steak*

Marinade:
1/2   *cup ginger ale*
1/2   *cup orange juice*
1/4   *cup firmly packed brown sugar*
1   *tablespoon vegetable oil*
1 1/2   *teaspoons white vinegar*
1   *teaspoon dry mustard*
1/4   *teaspoon ground ginger*
1/8   *teaspoon ground cloves*

Combine all of the marinade ingredients. Stir until sugar has dissolved. Pour over ham, cover and marinade for 8 hours. Drain the ham and discard marinade.

Grill the ham at 350 degrees for 15 minutes on each side.

Yields: 4 servings

Karen Harris

◆ SPICY CREOLE ◆
PORK CHOPS

8   *center-cut loin pork chops, 5-ounces each, trimmed of fat*
1/4   *cup light brown sugar, firmly packed*
1/4   *cup Worcestershire sauce*
3   *tablespoons Creole seasoning (or less, to taste)*
2   *tablespoons vegetable oil*
1   *tablespoon cider vinegar*

Arrange pork chops in a single layer in a large, shallow baking dish and set aside.

In a small bowl, using a wire whisk or fork, beat the sugar, Worcestershire sauce, Creole seasoning, oil, and vinegar. Pour the mixture over the pork chops, turning to coat both sides. Let the pork chops stand at room temperature for 30 minutes or refrigerate up to 12 hours.

Heat the broiler, first positioning the rack about 6-inches from the heat source. Arrange chops on rack in broiler pan. Broil for 5 to 6 minutes on each side until lightly browned and cooked through.

Yields: 8 servings

Deborah Alston

♦ LEMON BUTTER ♦ PORK CHOPS

1	stick margarine
1/3	cup lemon juice
6	pork chops
	Salt and pepper

Preheat oven to 350 degrees. Melt the margarine in a pan and add lemon juice. Coat pork chop with margarine mixture. Season with salt and pepper and place pork chops in a 13x9-inch pan. Bake at 350 degrees for 30 to 35 minutes until done.

Yields: 6 servings

Betty Young

♦ DELICIOUS ♦
PORK TENDERLOIN

1 1/2 to 2	pounds pork tenderloin

Marinade:

1 1/2	cups salad oil
3/4	cup soy sauce
2	tablespoons dry mustard
1	tablespoon black pepper
1/3	cup fresh lemon juice
1/2	cup white wine vinegar
1 1/2	teaspoons minced fresh parsley
1	clove garlic, crushed

Combine the marinade ingredients and pour over meat. Cover and refrigerate 24 hours. Preheat oven 350 degrees or prepare grill.

Drain marinade from pork and reserve. Place tenderloin in broiler pan or on grill. Bake at 350 degrees for 30 to 45 minutes. Baste frequently.

Yields: 6 to 8 servings

Deborah Alston

◆ POULTRY AND FISH ◆

Charlie and Van Young

A handsome Marine corpsman poses with his dad, after returning home from World War II. In 1951, Charlie joined the family as Margaret's husband.

Since Granny's husband died before I was born, the only grandfather in my life was Van Young, my father's father. I will always remember Granddaddy as a boisterous, happy man who was always in charge. When we visited my grandparents in Jackson, Tennessee, Granddaddy would take me downtown to visit the stores and introduce me to his friends at the post office and library. I still have a treasured doll which he bought me on one of our expeditions. We always went to the library to bring home a few books that I could read while his St. Louis Cardinals were playing. Granddaddy had a strict rule that no one could talk while the Cardinals' ball game was on the radio. We weren't allowed to talk while the game was on even if he was asleep!

How I love that tall Marine next to Granddaddy! My Dad, Charlie, is the steady sea anchor to the high energy, racketing ship of the Allen sisters. A quiet and omnivorous reader, this man has always had the answers to all my questions.

♦ TARRAGON CHICKEN ♦

2	large carrots, peeled and cut into julienne strips
2	stalks celery, cut into julienne strips
1	tablespoon margarine
1/4	teaspoon salt
1/8	teaspoon pepper
4	chicken breast halves, skinned and boned
1/4	cup all-purpose flour
1	teaspoon salt
1/4	teaspoon pepper
1/4	cup margarine
3/4	teaspoon dried crushed tarragon
1/2	cup dry white wine

Cook carrots and celery in a small amount of boiling water for 5 minutes until crisp-tender. Drain and return to saucepan. Stir in the 1 tablespoon margarine, salt, and pepper; set aside and keep warm.

Place each piece of chicken between 2 sheets of wax paper, and flatten to 1/4-inch thickness using a meat mallet. Combine the flour, salt, and pepper; dredge the chicken in flour mixture. Melt the remaining margarine in a large skillet over medium heat. Add the chicken, and cook 3 to 4 minutes on each side or until golden brown. Remove the chicken, reserving drippings in skillet. Drain the chicken on paper towels; keep the chicken warm.

Add the tarragon and wine to pan drippings, stirring well. Arrange the vegetables on individual serving plates; place chicken on top of vegetables. Spoon wine sauce over vegetables and chicken.

Yields: 4 servings

Karen Harris

◆ CHICKEN BAKE ◆

4	boneless chicken breasts
	Dijon mustard
3	tablespoons margarine or butter, melted
1	medium onion, sliced
2	zucchini, sliced
2	yellow squash, sliced
1/4	pound mushrooms, sliced
	Cooking spray
2/3	teaspoon basil
1	clove garlic, chopped
1/8	teaspoon paprika
1/2	cup grated Parmesan cheese

Preheat oven to 400 degrees. Brush mustard on the chicken. Brush the margarine on the onions, zucchini, squash and mushrooms. In a small bowl, mix the basil, garlic, paprika and cheese.

Spray a large piece of aluminum foil with cooking spray. Place the chicken on the aluminum foil. Sprinkle portion of cheese mixture on the chicken. Place the onions, zucchini, squash and mushrooms on chicken. Sprinkle remaining cheese mixture on vegetables. Fold the foil to create enclosed packet for baking. Place packet in (uncovered) pan for baking .

Bake at 400 degrees for 18 to 20 minutes.

Yields: 4 servings

Margaret Young

♦ OVEN-GLAZED ♦ CHICKEN

4	*skinless chicken breast halves*
1	*11 1/8-ounce can Campbell's Italian tomato soup*
2	*tablespoons water*
2	*tablespoons vinegar*
1	*tablespoon packed brown sugar*
1	*tablespoon Worcestershire sauce*

Preheat oven to 375 degrees. In a 2-quart baking dish, arrange the chicken. Bake at 375 degrees for 30 minutes. While the chicken cooks, combine the soup, water, vinegar, brown sugar and Worcestershire sauce in a small bowl. Mix and set aside. Spoon the soup mixture over the chicken. Bake at 375 degrees for an additional 30 minutes. Stir sauce before serving.

Yields: 4 servings

Pat Rush

◆ CHICKEN AND WINE ◆

4   *chicken breast halves or 1 chicken, quartered*
4   *tablespoons margarine or butter*
1   *cup chopped onion*
3/4 *cup chopped celery*
1 1/2 *cups white wine*

In a heavy skillet, lightly brown the chicken in heated margarine. Remove the chicken. Add the onion and celery to skillet; cook until tender but not brown. Stir in the wine. Return the chicken to skillet. Cover and cook for 1 hour, basting a several times with the sauce.

Yields: 4 servings

Karen Harris

◆ CHICKEN BREAST IN ◆
MUSHROOM WINE SAUCE

2   *tablespoons vegetable oil*
4   *skinless, boneless chicken breast halves*
2   *cups sliced mushrooms*
1   *11 1/8-ounce can Campbell's Italian tomato soup*
1/2   *cup water*
2   *tablespoons Burgundy or other dry red wine*
        Hot cooked noodles or rice

In a skillet, add 1 tablespoon oil and the chicken. Cook over medium-high heat or until browned on both sides. Remove chicken and set aside. Add the remaining oil and mushrooms, and cook until tender and liquid is evaporated, stirring occasionally. Stir in the soup, water, and wine. Heat to boiling. Return chicken to skillet. Reduce heat to low. Cover and cook for 5 minutes, until chicken is no longer pink, stirring occasionally. Serve over noodles or rice.

Yields: 4 servings

Pat Rush

♦ CHICKEN ♦
BREASTS DIANA

4	*large boneless chicken breast halves*
1/2	*teaspoon salt*
1/4 to 1/2	*teaspoon black pepper*
2	*tablespoons olive or salad oil*
2	*tablespoons margarine or butter*
3	*tablespoons chopped chives or green onions*
	Juice of 1/2 lime or lemon
2	*tablespoons brandy or cognac, optional*
3	*tablespoons chopped parsley*
2	*teaspoons Dijon mustard*
1/4	*cup chicken broth*

Place the chicken breasts between sheets of waxed paper and pound slightly with a mallet. Sprinkle with salt and black pepper.

Heat 1 tablespoon each of oil and margarine in a large skillet. Cook the chicken over high meat for 4 minutes on each side. Do not cook longer or meat will be overcooked and dry. Transfer the chicken to a warm serving dish.

Add the chives or onions, lime juice, brandy, parsley and mustard to the pan. Cook 15 seconds, whisking constantly. Add the chicken broth and whisk. Add the remaining oil and margarine and whisk. Pour the sauce over chicken and serve immediately.

Yields: 4 servings

Pat Rush

◆ CHICKEN-FRIED ◆
WILD RICE

1	pound skinned, boned chicken breasts
1/4	cup low-sodium teriyaki sauce
1/4	cup low-sodium soy sauce
1/4	cup Chablis or other dry white wine
2	cloves garlic, minced
1/2	teaspoon peeled, grated ginger root
1/4	teaspoon Chinese five-spice powder
1	4-ounce package uncooked wild rice
1	teaspoon vegetable oil
1	cup sliced green pepper
2/3	cup sliced carrot
2/3	cup chopped onion
2/3	cup sliced fresh mushrooms
1/2	cup frozen English peas, thawed
2	tablespoons slivered almonds, toasted

Cut the chicken into 1-inch pieces. Add the teriyaki sauce, soy sauce, wine, garlic, ginger root, and five-spice power. Stir well. Cover and marinate in the refrigerator at least 1 hour.

Cook the rice according to package directions, omitting the salt; and keep warm. Add oil to a wok or heavy skillet, and heat to medium high for 1 minute. Add the green pepper, carrots, and onions and stir-fry for 3 minutes. Add the mushrooms and peas and stir-fry for 2 minutes. Stir the vegetables into the rice and set aside. Coat the wok with cooking spray and place over medium-high heat until hot. Add the chicken and marinade to wok; stir-fry for 4 minutes or until done. Add the rice and stir-fry for 1 to 2 minutes or until heated. Sprinkle with almonds.

Yields: 4 servings

Pat Rush

◆ CHICKEN AND ◆ MUSHROOM RICE CASSEROLE

Easy to prepare and good!

1	box chicken Rice-A-Roni
4	chicken breasts
1	can of golden mushroom soup
	Fresh mushrooms, sliced
1	package Lipton dried onion soup

Prepare the Rice-A-Roni according to the package's directions, but cook the rice only half of the stated time. Preheat oven to 350 degrees.

Place the rice in the bottom of a casserole dish. Lay the chicken breasts on top of rice. Place the sliced mushrooms over chicken. Pour the undiluted soup over chicken. Sprinkle the soup mix over the soup . Bake at 350 degrees for 1 hour.

Yields: 4 servings

Libby Brown

◆ CHICKEN IN ◆
MUSHROOM SAUCE

8	chicken breasts, skinned
1	stick margarine
8	mushrooms, sliced
1/4	teaspoon salt
1/3	cup all-purpose flour
1	13 3/4-ounce can chicken broth
2	tablespoons light cream

In a large skillet, brown both sides of the chicken breast in 6 tablespoons of margarine over medium high heat. Place chicken on warm platter and set aside.

Add the mushrooms and 2 tablespoons margarine to the skillet and cook over medium heat, until mushrooms are golden brown. Place mushrooms on the platter.

Stir salt and flour into drippings until blended. Stir in chicken broth and cream, cook simmering over medium heat until thick and smooth. Place chicken and mushrooms into sauce. Simmer about 1 hour covered until fork tender.

Yields: 8 servings

Margaret Young

♦ Mushroom Chicken ♦

2	tablespoons oil
1	tablespoon margarine or butter
1 to 2	teaspoons Worcestershire sauce
1/4	cup wine
1	package skinless, boneless chicken
	All-purpose flour
1	can sliced mushrooms

Pour the oil into a medium hot pan, add the margarine and Worcestershire sauce, and wine. After washing the chicken, lightly flour and put in pan. Let the chicken brown, then add the mushrooms and cover. Reduce to medium heat and cook slowly for about 20 minutes. Add water if the sauce gets too thick.

Yields: 8 servings

Sharon Mack

♦ CHICKEN IN WINE ♦ AND MUSHROOM SAUCE

12	boneless chicken breasts
	Salt and pepper to taste
1	stick butter, melted
1	pound of fresh mushrooms, sliced
1/2	cup of white wine
6	tablespoons all-purpose flour
	White rice or wild rice, cooked

Preheat oven to 350 degrees. Season the chicken with salt and pepper. Fold under edges of chicken. Place in baking pan and bake uncovered at 350 degrees for 35 minutes.

Melt butter and saute the mushrooms until tender, about 2 minutes. Pour the juices from the chicken into the mushrooms. Add the flour to the wine and stir into the mushroom mixture. Cook until thick.

Pour the mushroom mixture over the chicken. Cover with foil and bake at 350 degrees for 20 to 25 minutes, or until chicken is done. Serve with rice, using mushroom mixture as gravy.

Yields: 12 servings

Margaret Young

◆ CHICKEN DIVAN ◆

Chicken:
2   9-ounce packages frozen broccoli
6   chicken breast halves cooked, skinned, and cut in chunks
2   10 1/2 ounce cans cream of chicken soup
1/2   cup milk
1/2   cup mayonnaise
1/2   teaspoon curry powder
1   teaspoon lemon juice
1   cup sharp cheese, grated

Topping:
1/2   cup stuffing mix
1/2   cup bread crumbs
2   tablespoons margarine, melted

To prepare the chicken: Preheat oven to 350 degrees. Cook the broccoli and drain. Arrange in a 9x13-inch casserole, with florets at edge of dish and stalks toward the center. Arrange the chicken over the broccoli. Combine the soup, milk, mayonnaise, curry powder, lemon juice, and cheese and pour over the broccoli and chicken.

To prepare the topping: Combine the stuffing mix, bread crumbs, and margarine and sprinkle over the chicken. Bake at 350 degrees for 40 minutes or until bubbly.

Note: The chicken can be made ahead and frozen. Prepare the topping at the time of serving.

Yields: 10 servings

Eleanor Helms

◆ CHICKEN PICCATA ◆

Chicken:

6	*boneless and skinless chicken breasts*
2	*tablespoons all-purpose flour*
2	*tablespoons margarine*
2	*tablespoons olive oil*
1	*can mushroom pieces*
1	*can chicken broth*
1/4	*cup marsala wine*
	Salt and pepper to taste
1 to 2	*tablespoons lemon juice*

Rice Pilaf:

1	*package brown rice*
1	*can chicken broth*
	Pine nuts or almonds, optional

To prepare the chicken: Flatten chicken to 1/4-inch thickness using a meat mallet or rolling pin. Dredge the chicken in the flour. In a frying pan, saute the chicken in butter and oil. Remove the chicken from the pan. Saute the mushrooms and remove from the pan. Sprinkle flour in the drippings and brown. Remove the pan from the heat, and add chicken broth and marsala wine. Add salt and pepper to taste. Add the lemon juice, chicken and mushrooms to pan. Simmer to reheat.

To prepare the rice: Cook brown rice according to package directions, substituting chicken broth for water. After the rice is cooked, add pine nuts or almonds. Salt and pepper to taste.

Yields: 6 servings

Eleanor Helms

◆ CHICKEN MARSALA ◆

A treat for family and guests.

6	whole boned chicken breasts
3	eggs, well beaten
	Seasoned bread crumbs
3	tablespoons oil
1	pound fresh mushrooms, sliced
2	cloves garlic, minced
1	10 1/2-ounce can chicken broth
1/3	cup marsala wine
1	3-ounce package mozzarella cheese, grated

Cut the chicken breasts into strips. Place the chicken in a bowl with the beaten eggs. Marinate overnight or at least 4 hours.

Preheat oven to 350 degrees. Coat the chicken with bread crumbs. Brown the chicken in the oil. Alternate the chicken with the mushrooms in a 9x13-inch casserole. Combine the garlic, chicken broth, and wine. Pour over chicken.

Bake, covered, at 350 degrees for 30 minutes. Bake uncovered for 15 minutes. Top the chicken with cheese and cook uncovered for 15 minutes.

Yields: 6 servings

Eleanor Helms

♦ CHICKEN TETRAZZINI ♦

Easy recipe to prepare for those
covered dish dinners.

1	7-ounce package vermicelli spaghetti or noodles
1	cup chicken stock
1	hen, boiled and cut into bite-size pieces
1	large onion, diced
1	green pepper, diced
1	cup celery, diced
1/4	cup butter or margarine
2	10 3/4-ounce cans cream of mushroom soup
2	cups grated cheese
1/2 to 1	cup slivered almonds

Preheat oven to 375 degrees. Cook the spaghetti in chicken stock. Drain and reserve 1/2 cup of the stock. Saute the onion, green pepper and celery in butter until soft. Grease the bottom of a 2-quart casserole. Cover with half of the chicken and half of the onion/celery mixture. Salt this to taste and pour 1/4 cup of chicken stock over the mixture. Add 1 can of soup. Make another layer using the remainder of the chicken, cooked spaghetti, vegetable mixture, 1/4 cup chicken stock and 1 can soup. Top with grated cheese and almonds.

Bake, covered, at 375 degrees for 30 to 45 minutes. Can be prepared in advance and refrigerated.

Yields: 8 servings

Jackie Brown
Eleanor Helms

◆ Chicken Mornay ◆

2	whole chicken breasts (4 halves), skinned and boned
4	tablespoons butter or margarine
2	tablespoons all-purpose flour
1	cup milk
1/4	teaspoon salt
1/8	teaspoon freshly ground white pepper
	Dash cayenne
1/4	cup plus 2 tablespoons grated Parmesan
1/4	cup grated Swiss or Gruyere cheese

Pound chicken between sheets of waxed paper to flatten evenly. Heat 2 tablespoons of the butter in a large, nonstick skillet. Add chicken in a single layer. Brown both sides, about 3 minutes. Cover and cook for 3 more minutes, until juices run clear. Remove from heat.

Heat the broiler. Melt the remaining 2 tablespoons butter in a small saucepan. Stir in flour; cook and stir 1 minute over medium heat. Whisk in milk, salt, pepper, and cayenne. Cook, stirring constantly, 3 minutes, until smooth and thick. Remove from heat. Stir in 1/4 cup Parmesan and the Swiss or Gruyere cheese until melted. Taste and adjust seasoning.

Pour sauce over chicken. Sprinkle with remaining 2 tablespoons Parmesan. Cook under the broiler for 2 to 3 minutes, or until lightly browned.

Yields: 4 servings

Karen Harris

◆ CHICKEN ◆
SALTIMBOCCA

3	large chicken breasts, skinned, boned and halved
6	thin slices boiled ham
3	slices mozzarella cheese, halved
1	medium tomato, seeded and chopped
1/2	teaspoon dried crushed sage
1/3	cup dried fine bread crumbs
2	tablespoons Parmesan cheese
2	tablespoons snipped parsley
4	tablespoons margarine, melted

Preheat oven to 350 degrees. Cover each chicken half with plastic wrap, pound lightly with meat mallet to 5x5-inches. Place a ham slice and half cheese slice on each cutlet, cutting to fit. Top with some tomato and dash of sage. Tuck in the sides and roll up jelly-roll style, pressing to seal well. Combine bread crumbs, parmesan and parsley. Dip chicken in margarine and roll in crumbs. Place in a shallow baking pan.

Bake at 350 degrees for 40 to 45 minutes.

Yields: 6 servings

Martha Helms

♦ CLAY-POT CHICKEN ♦

1	*chicken fryer, cut up or an equal amount of chicken parts*
1/4	*cup all purpose flour*
1/2	*teaspoon oregano*
1	*teaspoon paprika*
1/2	*teaspoon marjoram*
1/2	*teaspoon garlic salt*
2	*tablespoons olive oil*
	Salt to taste
	Pepper to taste
4	*green onions, diced*
12 to 18	*mushrooms, thinly sliced*
1/4	*cup dry white wine*
1/2	*pint sour cream, divided*
1/4	*pound Swiss cheese, shredded*

Presoak clay pot, top and bottom, in water for fifteen minutes. Shake chicken in bag containing mixture of flour, oregano, paprika, marjoram and garlic salt. Set aside any remaining seasoned flour.

Brown chicken in frying pan quickly in olive oil, adding salt and pepper to taste. Place browned chicken in pot, and add diced onions and sliced mushrooms.

To chicken drippings in saucepan, add white wine and 1/4 pint sour cream; heat and thicken with the remaining seasoned flour. Pour over chicken. Salt and pepper to taste. Sprinkle grated Swiss cheese over chicken.

Place covered pot in *cold* oven. Set temperature to 480 degrees and bake for 45 minutes. Remove from oven, pour off sauce into saucepan and thicken with 1/4 pint sour cream and flour, if needed.

Serve the sauce with the chicken or over rice.

Yields: 6 to 8 servings

Karen Harris

◆ APRICOT-MUSTARD ◆ CHICKEN

1	tablespoon margarine, melted
2	tablespoons oil
8	chicken breasts, skinned
1/2	cup all-purpose flour
	Salt to taste
1/2	cup apricot preserves
1	tablespoon Dijon mustard
1/2	cup nonfat yogurt
2	tablespoons slivered almonds

Preheat oven to 375 degrees. Place the margarine and oil in large baking dish. Dredge the chicken in flour and salt and shake off excess flour. Place a single layer of chicken in prepared casserole dish. Bake at 375 degrees for 25 minutes.

Combine apricot preserves, mustard and yogurt. Spread over chicken and bake an additional 30 minutes. Top with toasted almonds.

Yields: 8 servings

Sharon Mack

♦ ROAST ALMOND ♦ CHICKEN

10 to 12	chicken breast halves
	Salt and pepper
1	5-ounce package slivered or sliced almonds
1	10 3/4-ounce can cream of mushroom soup
1	10 3/4-ounce can cream of chicken soup
1	10 3/4-ounce can cream of celery soup
1/4	cup dry white wine
	Parmesan cheese

Preheat oven to 350 degrees. Wash the chicken breasts, remove the skin and pat dry with paper towels. Lightly salt and pepper the pieces and put into a buttered 13x9-inch baking dish. Cover with 2/3 of the almonds.

Combine the mushroom, chicken and celery soups. Mix the soups with the wine and pour over chicken. Sprinkle generously with Parmesan cheese and remainder of almonds and bake, covered with foil, at 350 degrees for 2 hours. May be prepared ahead and heated at the last minute.

Yields: 6 to 8 servings

Eleanor Helms

◆ PARTY CHICKEN ◆

8	large chicken breasts, skinned and deboned
8	slices bacon, uncooked
1	small jar dried chipped beef
1	10 3/4-ounce can cream of mushroom soup
1/2	pint sour cream
1	small can sliced mushrooms

Wrap each breast in bacon. Cover bottom of a flat greased baking dish with chipped beef. Place chicken breasts in dish. Mix the soup, sour cream and mushrooms, and pour over the chicken. Bake at 275 degrees, uncovered, for 3 hours.

Yields: 8 servings

Deborah Alston

◆ CHICKEN ROLLUPS ◆ IN GRAVY

6   chicken breasts, skinned and boned
1   teaspoon garlic powder
1/2   teaspoon salt
1/2   teaspoon pepper
        Flour
6   slices of ham
6   slices of Swiss cheese
2   tablespoons vegetable oil
1 1/2   cups chicken broth
1   can cream of chicken soup
1   can sliced mushrooms, undrained
        Hot cooked rice

Place chicken on waxed paper; flatten to 1/4 inch thickness with a mallet or rolling pin. Sprinkle both sides of chicken with garlic powder, salt, and pepper, and dredge in flour.

Place a slice of ham and cheese in the center of each chicken breast. Roll up lengthwise and secure with a wooden toothpick. Brown the chicken in hot oil. Combine the chicken broth, soup and mushrooms. Pour the soup mixture over the chicken. Cover, reduce heat and simmer 30 minutes. Serve over rice.

Yields: 6 servings

Debbie Brown

◆ SAVORY CRESCENT ◆ CHICKEN SQUARES

1	3-ounce package cream cheese, softened
3	tablespoons margarine or butter, melted
2	cups cooked cubed chicken or two 5-ounce cans boned chicken
1/4	teaspoon salt
1/8	teaspoon pepper
2	tablespoons milk
1	tablespoon chopped chives or onion
1	teaspoon Nature's Seasons or other all-purpose seasoning spice
1	tablespoon chopped pimento, optional
1	8-ounce can refrigerated crescent dinner rolls
3/4	cup seasoned croutons, crushed

Preheat oven to 350 degrees. In medium bowl, blend cream cheese and 2 tablespoons margarine until smooth. Add the chicken, salt, pepper, milk, chives or onion, seasoning spice and pimento, if used. Mix well.

Separate crescent dough into 4 rectangles; firmly press perforations to seal.

Spoon approximately 1/2 cup chicken mixture onto center of each rectangle. Pull 4 corners of dough to top center of chicken mixture, twist slightly and seal edges. Brush tops with remaining 1 tablespoon margarine; sprinkle crouton crumbs on top of each square.

Place on ungreased baking sheet. Bake at 350 degrees for 20 to 25 minutes.

Yields: 4 servings

Deborah Alston

♦ BUTTERMILK ♦
PECAN CHICKEN

1	cup buttermilk
1	egg, slightly beaten
1	tablespoon paprika
1/8	teaspoon pepper
1	cup all-purpose flour
1	cup ground pecans
1/4	cup sesame seeds
1	tablespoon salt
2	2 1/2 to 3 1/2 pound fryers, cut up
1/2	cup corn oil
1/4	cup chopped pecans

Preheat oven to 350 degrees. Combine the buttermilk and egg in a small bowl. Combine the paprika, pepper, flour, ground pecans, sesame seeds and salt in a separate bowl. Dip chicken in the buttermilk mixture and then in the seasoning mixture. Quickly dip the chicken in the in oil, let drip, place on a roasting pan with skin sides up. Sprinkle with finely chopped nuts. Bake at 350 degrees for 1 1/4 to 2 hours.

Yields: 8 servings

Margaret Young

◆ CHICKEN & STUFFING ◆

1	6-ounce package chicken flavored stuffing mix
1/2	cup chopped carrot
1/2	cup celery
1/2	cup onion
1	10 3/4-ounce can cream of mushroom soup
1/3	cup milk
1	teaspoon chopped parsley
6	skinless, boneless chicken breast halves
	Paprika to taste

Preheat oven to 400 degrees. Prepare stuffing mix according to package directions, and add vegetables with the seasoning packet. In a small bowl, combine the soup, milk and parsley; set aside.

In a 2-quart baking dish, arrange stuffing across center of dish. Spoon thin layer of the soup mixture in casserole on each side of stuffing. Arrange chicken over soup mixture; overlap if necessary. Sprinkle with paprika.

Pour the remaining soup mixture over the chicken. Cover with foil and bake 15 minutes at 400 degrees. Uncover and bake for 10 minutes, until chicken is fork-tender. Stir sauce before serving.

Yields: 6 servings

Karen Harris

◆CHAMPAGNE CHICKEN◆

2	tablespoons margarine or butter
4	chicken breast halves, skinned and boned
1/2	cup sliced fresh mushrooms
1/3	cup champagne
1/3	cup sour cream
1/8	teaspoon salt
1/8	teaspoon white pepper

Preheat oven to 350 degrees. Heat margarine in a medium skillet. Add the chicken, and brown on both sides. Remove the chicken to a 1-quart baking dish, reserving drippings in skillet. Add the mushrooms to the skillet and saute; remove the mushrooms, and set aside.

Stir the champagne into drippings in skillet; simmer until thoroughly heated, stirring occasionally. Pour over the chicken; cover and bake at 350 degrees for 20 minutes or until chicken is done.

Remove the chicken to the platter, reserving liquid. Add sour cream, salt, and pepper to reserved liquid; whisk until smooth. Pour over the chicken, and top with mushrooms.

Yield: 2 servings

Karen Harris

♦ HAWAIIAN CHICKEN ♦

1   whole chicken, cut-up
1/2   cup teriyaki sauce
1   48-ounce can pineapple juice

Remove the skin from the chicken. Poke the chicken pieces with a fork. Mix the juice and teriyaki in a large bowl, and add the chicken. Marinate in refrigerator for 6 hours or overnight.

Preheat oven to 350 degrees. Place the chicken in a large broiler pan and bake for 40 minutes at 350 degrees.

Yield: 6 servings

Betty Young

♦ CHICKEN ♦
CONTINENTAL

3	pounds frying chicken, cut-up
1/4	cup all-purpose flour
2	tablespoons salad oil
1	4-ounce can sliced mushrooms
1	16-ounce can tomatoes, chopped
1/3	cup soy sauce
1	clove garlic, minced
1	medium onion, sliced
1/4	cup sliced pitted black olives, optional
3	cups hot cooked rice, cooked according to package directions

Coat the chicken pieces thoroughly with flour; brown slowly in hot oil. Meanwhile, drain mushrooms, reserving liquid. Combine the mushroom liquid with tomatoes, soy sauce and garlic. Add the tomato mixture and onion to the chicken and stir. Cover and simmer 45 minutes, or until chicken is tender. Stir in mushrooms and olives; bring to boil. Serve over fluffy rice.

Yields: 4 to 6 servings

Karen Harris

♦ CHICKEN AND ♦ VEGETABLE PASTA

2	*tablespoons margarine*
4	*chicken breasts*
1	*squash, sliced*
1	*zucchini, sliced*
1	*14-ounce can artichoke hearts, drained*
6 to 10	*shittake mushrooms, sliced*
1	*onion, sliced*
1	*14 1/2-ounce can stewed tomatoes, Italian recipe with basil, garlic nd oregano*
1	*8-ounce can tomato sauce*
1	*6-ounce can tomato paste*
	Penne style pasta
1/2	*cup whipping cream*
	Pasta

In a frying pan, brown the chicken in margarine for 4 to 5 minutes on each side. Remove the chicken and keep warm. Saute the squash, zucchini, onion, mushrooms and artichoke hearts. Add the chicken to the vegetables. Add tomato sauce, tomato paste and cream. Simmer for 15 to 20 minutes. Serve over cooked pasta.

Yields: 4 servings

Libby Brown

♦ BARBECUED CHICKEN ♦

6	skinless, boneless chicken breast halves
1/4	cup vinegar
1/2	cup water
1/4	cup margarine
2	tablespoons sugar
1 1/2	teaspoons salt
1	thick slice lemon
1	onion, peeled and sliced
1	tablespoon mustard
1/2	teaspoon pepper
1/2	cup ketchup
2	tablespoons Worcestershire sauce

Preheat oven to 350 degrees. Place chicken in a 1-quart baking dish.

Mix the vinegar, water, margarine, sugar, salt, lemon, onion, mustard and pepper in a saucepan. Simmer 20 minutes uncovered. Add the ketchup and Worcestershire sauce. Bring to a boil. Pour over chicken. Bake at 350 degrees for 1 hour.

Yields: 6 servings

Eleanor Helms

♦ SKILLET HERB ♦
ROASTED CHICKEN

2	tablespoons all-purpose flour
1/4	teaspoon ground sage
1/4	teaspoon dried thyme
4	skinless, boneless chicken breast halves
2	tablespoons margarine
1	10 3/4-ounce can cream of chicken soup
1/4	cup water
	Hot cooked rice

On waxed paper, combine the flour, sage and thyme. Coat the chicken lightly with flour mixture.

In a skillet over medium-high heat, cook the chicken in the margarine for 10 minutes, or until browned on both sides; push the chicken to one side.

Stir in soup and water, stirring to loosen browned bits. Reduce heat to low. Cover and simmer for 10 minutes or until chicken is fork-tender. Serve over rice. Garnish with fresh thyme if desired.

Yields: 4 servings

Karen Harris

♦ CAJUN-SPICE ♦
RICE SKILLET

2	tablespoons margarine
1	pound skinless, boneless chicken breasts, cut into 1 1/2-inch pieces
1	medium green pepper, chopped
1	medium onion, chopped
1/2	teaspoon paprika
1/2	teaspoon dried oregano
1/4	teaspoon ground red pepper
1/4	teaspoon black pepper
1	10 3/4-ounce can Campbell's golden corn soup
1	16-ounce can stewed tomatoes, cut up
1	cup cooked rice

In a skillet, add 1 tablespoon margarine and half of the chicken. Over medium-high heat, cook the chicken for approximately 10 minutes, until brown on both sides and remove from pan. Add 1 tablespoon margarine and the remaining chicken to the skillet. Cook the chicken for 10 minutes until browned on both sides and remove from pan. Spoon off fat from the pan.

In the same skillet, add 1 tablespoon margarine, green pepper and onion, paprika, oregano, and peppers. Cook vegetables until tender-crisp, stirring occasionally. Add the soup, tomatoes and rice to the vegetable mixture. Heat to boiling. Return the chicken to the skillet. Reduce heat to low, cover, and cook for 5 minutes until chicken is no longer pink.

Yields: 4 servings

Pat Rush

♦ SKILLET ♦
CORN CHICKEN

1	tablespoon margarine
4	skinless, boneless chicken breast halves
1	10 3/4-ounce can Campbell's golden corn soup
1/2	cup milk
2	cups broccoli florets
1/2	cup shredded Cheddar cheese
1/8	teaspoon pepper

In a skillet, add the margarine and chicken. Over medium-high heat, cook the chicken for 10 minutes, until both sides are browned. Remove chicken and set aside. Spoon off the fat from the pan.

Stir in the soup, milk, broccoli, cheese and pepper. Heat to boiling. Return chicken to the skillet. Reduce heat to low. Cover and cook for 10 minutes, until the chicken is no longer pink and broccoli is tender-crisp. Stir occasionally.

Yields: 4 servings

Pat Rush

◆ BAKED ◆
CHICKEN NUGGETS

1/2	cup fine dry bread crumbs
1/4	cup grated Parmesan cheese
1/4	teaspoon salt
1/2	teaspoon basil
1/2	teaspoon thyme
4	chicken breast halves, skinned and boned
1/4	cup butter or margarine, melted

Preheat the oven to 400 degrees. Combine the bread crumbs, Parmesan cheese, salt, basil and thyme in a plastic bag; shake well.

Cut the chicken into 1-inch pieces; dip chicken pieces in butter, and shake a few at a time in the bread crumb mixture. Place on a lightly greased baking sheet. Bake at 400 degrees for 20 minutes or until tender.

Yields: 4 servings

Margaret Young

♦OVEN FRIED CHICKEN♦

1	tablespoon margarine
2/3	cup Bisquick baking mix
1 1/2	teaspoons paprika
1 1/4	teaspoons salt
1/4	teaspoon pepper
2 1/2 to 3 1/2	pound chicken fryer, skinned and cut-up

Preheat oven to 400 degrees. Melt margarine in 13x9-inch pan or baking dish. In a bowl, mix the Bisquick, paprika, salt and pepper. Coat chicken and place fat side down in pan. Bake for 35 minutes at 400 degrees. Turn the chicken pieces and bake 15 to 20 minutes or until well done.

Yields: 6 servings

Ida Helms

◆ SPINACH AND ◆ CHICKEN CASSEROLE

10	ounces rigatoni
1	10-ounce package frozen chopped spinach, thawed
	Vegetable cooking spray
2/3	cup chopped onion
2	cloves garlic, minced
1	pound boneless chicken breasts, skinned, and cut into 1-inch pieces
2	14 1/2 ounce cans whole tomatoes, undrained and coarsely chopped
3	tablespoons tomato paste
1 1/4	teaspoons basil
3/4	teaspoon oregano
1/4	teaspoon crushed red pepper
1/2	cup grated Parmesan cheese, divided

Cook the pasta according to package directions and drain. Preheat oven to 350 degrees. Place the spinach on paper towels and pat dry.

Add oil and heat skillet on medium high. Add the onion and garlic and saute until tender. Add the chicken and cook until no longer pink. Stir in the tomatoes, tomato paste, basil, oregano, and pepper. Bring to a boil. Reduce heat and simmer 5 minutes.

Spray a 13x9-inch baking dish with vegetable spray. Combine the pasta, spinach, chicken mixture and 1/4 cup cheese in a bowl. Spoon the mixture into the baking dish. Sprinkle with remaining cheese. Bake at 350 degrees for 20 minutes or until thoroughly heated.

Yields: 4 to 6 servings

Sharon Mack

◆ CHICKEN ◆
MARSEILLAISE

1	*2 1/2 to 3-pound broiler-fryer, cut up*
2/3	*cup Catalina French Dressing*
1	*16-ounce can tomatoes*
8	*onion slices, 1/4 inch thick*
1	*teaspoon salt*
1/2	*teaspoon celery seed*
1/4	*teaspoon pepper*
1/4	*cup dry white wine or water*
2	*tablespoons all-purpose flour*

Brown chicken in 1/3 cup dressing over low heat in a skillet. Add the remaining dressing, tomatoes, onion, salt, celery seed and pepper. Cover and simmer for 45 minutes. Remove chicken and vegetables to a serving platter and keep warm.

Gradually add the wine to flour, stirring until well blended. Gradually add flour mixture to hot liquid in pan; cook and stir constantly. Serve as gravy for chicken and vegetables.

Yields: 4 servings

Karen Harris

♦ Chicken Casserole ♦

4 to 6   *chicken breasts or 1 chicken*
2   *10 3/4-ounce cans cream of chicken soup*
2   *cans water*
1   *8-ounce package stuffing crumbs*

Preheat oven to 350 degrees. Boil the chicken until done. Remove the chicken from the bone and cut into bite-size pieces; season to taste. Place the chicken in a 9x13-inch pan. Mix soup and water and pour over chicken. Top with stuffing crumbs.

Bake at 350 degrees for 20 minutes, until hot and top is browned.

Yields: 4 to 6 servings

Janet Allen

◆ CHICKEN AND ◆
RICE CASSEROLE

Chicken:

1	cup diced cooked chicken
1	cup diced cooked celery
1	cup cooked rice
1	10 3/4-ounce can cream of chicken soup
2	tablespoons chopped onion
1/3	cup mayonnaise
1	can sliced water chestnuts
1/2	cup sliced almonds

Topping:

1	cup cornflakes crushed
1/4	stick margarine or butter, melted

Preheat oven to 350 degrees. Mix the chicken, celery, rice, soup, onion, mayonnaise, water chestnuts and almonds. Pour into a greased medium casserole.

Mix the cornflakes and margarine. Spread over the chicken mixture. Bake at 350 degrees for 45 minutes.

Yields: 4 to 6 servings

Eleanor Helms

♦ EASY ♦
CHICKEN CASSEROLE

6 to 7 chicken breasts, skinned, cooked and diced
1   can cream of celery soup
1/2   cup milk
1   stick margarine or butter, melted
1 1/2   cups Pepperidge Farms herb seasoned dressing mix

Preheat oven to 375 degrees. Place the chicken in the bottom of a casserole dish. Combine the celery soup and milk. Pour over the chicken. Combine the margarine and dressing. Cover chicken mixture with margarine and dressing mix.

Bake at 375 degrees for 20 minutes.

Yields: 4 to 6 servings

Eleanor Helms

♦ HURRY-UP ♦
CHICKEN STIR-FRY

2   *tablespoons vegetable oil, divided*
1   *cup broccoli florets*
1   *cup cauliflower florets*
1   *large carrot, peeled and cut into 2-inch strips*
3   *green onions, sliced*
1   *clove garlic, minced*
3   *skinned, boned chicken breast halves, cut into 1-inch pieces*
1/2   *cup Italian salad dressing*
1   *tablespoon soy sauce*
1/2   *teaspoon ground ginger*
       Hot cooked rice

Pour 1 tablespoon oil into wok or large skillet, coating the
bottom and sides. Heat to medium high for about 2 minutes.
Add broccoli, cauliflower, carrots, onions and garlic. Stir-fry for 4
minutes. Remove vegetables and set aside. Add 1 tablespoon oil
and chicken to pan. Stir-fry for 4 minutes or until tender. Return
vegetables to pan. Stir in salad dressing, soy sauce and ginger.
Serve over rice.

Yields: 3 servings

Pat Rush

◆ THANKSGIVING ◆
TURKEY AND GRAVY

While our family has enjoyed this recipe for many years, this is the first time it's been written down!

Turkey:

1	20 pound pre-basted turkey with thermometer
	Water
	Margarine or butter
1/8 to 1/4	cup salt
1	teaspoon flour
	Turkey cooking bag

Gravy:

	Juices from turkey, reserving juice required for Turkey Dressing (page 97)
	Pepper to taste
1 to 2	cans chicken broth
1/2	cup all-purpose flour
2	hard boiled eggs, coarse chopped
	Turkey giblets
2	tablespoons turkey dressing, optional

To prepare the turkey: If possible, thaw the turkey in the refrigerator for 4 to 5 days. If unable to refrigerate the turkey due to lack of space, leave turkey out until thawed but still cold. Preheat oven to 325 degrees. Remove the bag of giblets and neck from the turkey. Cook the giblets in water to cover and reserve for gravy.

Rinse the turkey. Spread margarine on the turkey breast and pour salt into the turkey cavity. Place the turkey on its back in a large cooking bag and put flour in the bottom of the bag. If you need to insert a thermometer, push the thermometer into the thickest part of the breast, insuring that it is not touching the bone.

Secure the bag and punch 4 to 6 holes in the top of the bag. Put the bag in the broiler pan and bake at 325 degrees until the meat thermometer shows 185 to 190 degrees. If using a turkey with its own thermometer, the thermometer will pop out when the turkey is done. When thermometer temperature reaches 185 degrees, remove the turkey and allow to cool. When bag is cool enough to touch, snip a small hole in the corner of the cooking bag and drain the turkey juices into a pot.

To prepare the gravy: Place the turkey juices into a large sauce pan and heat. Add pepper to taste. Blend the canned chicken broth and flour in a blender. Slowly pour the broth into the sauce pan, stirring until it thickens slightly. If the gravy is not thick enough, mix additional chicken broth and flour in blender and add to the sauce pan. After the gravy is slightly thickened, add the eggs. Cut the liver and gizzards into small pieces, removing tough or fatty parts. Add the turkey pieces to the gravy. Add the turkey dressing and mix well.

Yields: 20 to 22 servings

Gwen Allen

♦ BAKED FROZEN ♦
TURKEY BREAST

An easy way to bake a moist turkey breast.

1   *6-pound frozen turkey breast*
       Salt
       Onion salt
       Celery salt
       Accent
1   *tablespoon sugar*
2   *tablespoons melted margarine or butter*

Preheat oven to 450 degrees. Wash and dry the frozen breast. (Do not thaw). Season generously with salt, onion salt, celery salt, Accent and sugar.

Place turkey on heavy foil. Pour melted margarine over the breast. Wrap meat and overlap foil 3-4 inches. Fold up both ends. Place meat in shallow pan and roast at least 3 hours for 6 pound breast. Open foil and bake for 20 more minutes for browning.

Yields: 10 to 12 servings

Jackie Brown

◆ TURKEY POT PIE ◆

1	6-pound turkey
	Salt and pepper to taste
3	cups all-purpose flour
1	20-ounce package frozen mixed vegetables
1	teaspoon salt
2/3	cup vegetable shortening
8	tablespoons cold water

Boil the turkey until done, about 45 minutes. Retain the broth. Salt and pepper to taste. Remove the skin and remove the meat from the bone. Preheat oven to 350 degrees.

Combine the flour and salt. Cut in the shortening until the mixture resembles coarse meal. Slowly add the cold water to moisten. Knead the dough. Roll the pastry very thin and cut strips 2 1/2-inch wide.

Grease an 8x12x2-inch pan with margarine. Strip pastry across pan and up sides (without letting the strips touch). Put the meat in the pan. In a large saucepan, bring 5 cups broth to a boil; add the frozen vegetables and simmer for 10 minutes. Thicken the broth with flour. Pour the broth mixture over the meat. Lay pastry strips over top. Brush top with margarine.

Bake at 350 degrees for 30 to 45 minutes.

Yields: 10 to 12 servings

Jackie Brown

◆ FIVE CAN HOT DISH ◆

1	10 3/4-ounce can cream of mushroom soup
1	10 3/4-ounce can cream of chicken soup
1	6 1/8-ounce can tuna
1	5-ounce can evaporated milk
1	can chow mein noodles
1	cup finely chopped celery

Preheat oven to 350 degrees. Mix all ingredients. Bake in a casserole dish at 350 degrees for 1 hour.

Pat Rush

◆ SHRIMP AND ◆ RICE BAKE

2 1/2	pounds shrimp
3	10 1/2-ounce cans cream of mushroom soup
3/4	cup water
1	6-ounce box Uncle Ben's Long Grain and Wild Rice
1	large green pepper, chopped
1	2-ounce jar diced pimentos
2	cups finely chopped onion
1	cup finely chopped celery
1	pound cheddar cheese, shredded

Boil, peel and de-vein the shrimp. Preheat oven to 350 degrees. Dilute the soup with water. Cook rice according to package. Combine all ingredients. Pour into 3 quart casserole. Bake uncovered at 350 degrees for 45 minutes to 1 hour.

Yields: 8 servings

Deborah Alston

◆VEGETABLES ◆

December - Miss Eleanor Allen

MYERS PARK

1955 School Calendar

Eleanor is the family's cheerleader and calendar girl. I've always treasured her December 1955 calendar picture because I was born on Tuesday, December 13th of that year.

Eleanor went to the University of North Carolina, where she met a handsome fella, Parks Helms, during her freshman year. Over spring break, they married and returned to Chapel Hill the following year for Parks to attend UNC Law School. They led a "poor" but happy life in a small rental house on Friendly Lane.

Years later, Deborah (their daughter) and I both attended the University of North Carolina. During my years at "Blue Heaven," I was a charter member of the Alpha Chi Omega Sorority, which Deborah joined when she came to UNC. By chance, Alpha Chi built our sorority house next door to Eleanor and Parks' little rental house. When Parks visited Deborah at the sorority house, he always pulled back the curtain to stare, smiling, at that little house and reminisce about their happy days on Friendly Lane.

♦ ASPARAGUS ♦
PEA CASSEROLE

1	can asparagus, drained
1	can peas, drained with 3 tablespoons juice reserved
3	eggs, hard-boiled, sliced
1	10 3/4-ounce can cream of mushroom soup
12	saltine crackers, crumbled

Preheat oven to 350 degrees. Place the asparagus in a casserole dish and distribute peas and eggs evenly on top. Dilute the soup with the pea juice and pour over casserole. Spread the crackers over top.

Bake at 350 degrees for 30 minutes.

Yields: 4 to 6 servings

Jackie Brown

♦ASPARAGUS CASSEROLE♦

1	No. 2 can asparagus
1	10 3/4-ounce can cream of mushroom soup
2 1/2	cups cracker crumbs
1/2	pound grated cheese
2	hard-boiled eggs, sliced
1/2	stick margarine

Preheat oven to 350 degrees. Drain asparagus and mix liquid with soup. Mix cracker crumbs and cheese. In a 2-quart casserole dish, begin with a layer of crumbs and then layer with 1/2 the asparagus, then 1 egg sliced and 1/2 soup mixture. Repeat, ending with cracker-cheese mixture. Dot top with 1/2 stick margarine.

Bake at 350 degrees 20 minutes.

Yields: 4 to 6 servings

Eleanor Helms

◆ HEARTY BAKED BEANS ◆

1	pound ground chuck
2	cups chopped onions
2	16-ounce cans pork and beans
1	16-ounce can kidney beans
1	cup brown sugar
1	tablespoon vinegar
1	teaspoon salt
1	cup ketchup
1	tablespoon mustard

Preheat oven to 400 degrees. Brown the ground chuck and onions together and drain. Add the pork and beans, kidney beans, sugar, vinegar, salt, ketchup and mustard; mix well. Bake at 400 degrees for 30 to 40 minutes.

Yields: 8 to 10 servings

Karen Harris

◆ BAKED BEANS ◆

1	gallon can pork and beans
1/3 to 1/2	cup mustard
1 1/2 to 2	jars Grandma's molasses
2/3	cup ketchup
1/4	cup Worcestershire sauce
3/4	cup chopped onions

Preheat oven to 400 degrees. Combine the ingredients in a large pot. Bake at 400 degrees 1 hour covered. Uncover and bake an additional 20 minutes. If beans are soupy, stir and bake longer.

Yields: 20 to 25 servings

Eleanor Helms

◆ BROCCOLI CASSEROLE ◆

2	10-ounce packages frozen chopped broccoli
1	10 3/4-ounce can cream of mushroom soup
1/2	cup mayonnaise
1/2	cup minced fresh onion
1	cup grated sharp Cheddar cheese
2	beaten eggs
	Cheese cracker crumbs

Preheat oven to 400 degrees. Cook broccoli 5 minutes in boiling water and drain; put broccoli in colander and steam over boiling water for 10 minutes. Combine the mushroom soup, mayonnaise, onion, cheese, eggs and broccoli. Put in a 1 1/2-quart casserole dish and sprinkle with cheese cracker crumbs. Bake 20 minutes at 400 degrees.

Yields: 8 servings

Eleanor Helms

♦ SAUCY GOLDEN ♦ CORN AND BROCCOLI

1	1 1/2-pound bunch of broccoli, cut up
1	cup water
1	10 3/4-ounce Campbell's golden corn soup
1/4	cup milk
1/2	cup shredded Cheddar cheese
	Dash of pepper

In a 3-quart saucepan, combine the broccoli and water. Over high heat, bring water to boil. Reduce heat to low. Cover and cook 8 minutes or until broccoli is tender crisp. Stir occasionally. Drain in a colander.

In the same saucepan, stir the soup, milk, cheese and pepper. Return the broccoli to the saucepan. Heat thoroughly over medium heat, stirring occasionally.

Yields: 8 servings

Pat Rush

◆ CARROTS ◆

Colorful and delicious.

1	pound of carrots, sliced and cooked 20 minutes
1/2	cup sugar
1/2	cup orange juice
4	tablespoons margarine

Mix the sugar, orange juice and margarine. Pour the margarine mixture over carrots and cook on the stove top for 25 minutes, until tender.

Yields: 4 servings

Eleanor Helms

◆ CORN CASSEROLE ◆

2	cups fresh corn, cut from the ears
3/4	cup (3 ounces) shredded Swiss cheese
1/2	cup whipping cream
1	large egg, beaten
1/8	teaspoon salt
1/8	teaspoon pepper

Combine the corn, cheese, cream, egg, salt and pepper. Spoon into 4 lightly greased custard cups and bake at 350 degrees 20 to 25 minutes. Or, if using a greased 1-quart casserole, bake at 350 degrees for 30 to 35 minutes. Drain and serve warm.

Yields: 4 servings

Karen Harris

◆ CREAMY ◆
CARROT CASSEROLE

1 1/2   pound carrots, peeled and sliced
        Water to cover the carrots
1   cup mayonnaise
1   tablespoon grated onion
1   tablespoon prepared horseradish
1/4   cup shredded cheddar cheese
2   tablespoons buttered bread crumbs

Preheat oven to 350 degrees. In a saucepan, cook the carrots in water until crisp-tender. Drain, reserving 1/4 cup of the cooking liquid. Place the carrots in a 1 1/2-quart baking dish. Combine the mayonnaise, onion, horseradish and cooking liquid and spread the mayonnaise mixture evenly over carrots. Sprinkle with cheese and top with bread crumbs. Bake uncovered at 350 degrees for 30 minutes.

Yields: 8 to 10 servings   *Pat Rush*

♦ BAKED CORN ♦

2	cups corn, cooked
1	cup milk
2/3	cup cracker or bread crumbs
3	tablespoons margarine or butter, melted
1/2	teaspoon salt
1/8	teaspoon pepper
1	tablespoon sugar
2	eggs
1	teaspoon minced onion

Preheat oven to 350 degrees. Combine the corn, milk, bread crumbs, margarine, salt, pepper, sugar, eggs, and onion in a blender and mix lightly. Pour into a greased 1-quart casserole dish and bake at 350 degrees for 40 minutes.

Yields: 4 servings

Karen Harris

♦ TOKIKO'S ♦
CORN CASSEROLE

	Large box Jiffy cornbread mix
1	*large can whole kernel corn*
1	*large can creamed corn*
2	*eggs, slightly beaten*
1/2	*green pepper, chopped*
1	*medium onion, chopped*
1/2	*stick margarine or butter*
	Sour cream, optional
	Grated cheese

Preheat oven to 350 degrees. Mix together the cornbread mix, whole kernel corn, creamed corn and eggs. Pour the corn mixture into a casserole dish.

Saute the green pepper and onion in the margarine. Pour over the corn mixture. Top with sour cream, dropped by spoonfuls, and grated cheese.

Bake at 350 degrees for 25 to 30 minutes.

Yields: 4 to 6 servings

Patricia Weeks

♦ GRILLED EGGPLANT ♦

Tomato sauce:
4	small tomatoes, peeled, seeded and chopped
1/2	cup onion, chopped
1/4	cup chopped cilantro
1/4	cup vegetable oil or olive oil
1	lime juice
	Salt and pepper

Eggplant:
2	eggplants, peeled and sliced 1/2-inch thick
	Oil

Combine the tomatoes, onion, cilantro, oil, lime juice, salt and pepper. Mix well and refrigerate for 2 hours.

Place the oil into a skillet and grill the eggplant for 3 to 4 minutes on each side, turning 3 times. If desired, reheat the tomato sauce.

Serve eggplant hot with tomato sauce.

Yields: 4 servings

Margaret Young

♦ Eggplant ♦
Hollandale

2	large eggplants, peeled and diced
1	teaspoon sugar
1/2	cup chopped celery
3/4	cup chopped onion
1/2	green pepper, chopped
2	tablespoons margarine or butter
1	tablespoon parsley flakes
1	clove garlic, mashed, or garlic salt to taste
	Seasoned salt
	Tabasco
	Worcestershire sauce
1	large tomato, peeled and diced
1	7-ounce can shrimp or 1/2 pound peeled, cooked shrimp, optional
1	cup bread crumbs, divided (preferably Progresso)
1	egg beaten
3	tablespoons grated Parmesan cheese

Preheat oven to 350 degrees. Cook the eggplant in water seasoned with sugar until tender, about 10 minutes.

Saute the celery, onion and green pepper in butter until tender. Add the parsley, garlic, seasoned salt, Tabasco and Worcestershire sauce to taste. Mix the eggplant with sauteed vegetables, tomato, shrimp, 1/2 cup bread crumbs and egg.

Place the eggplant mixture in a casserole, and top with the remaining bread crumbs and Parmesan cheese; dot with additional butter. Cook at 350 degrees for 30 minutes. Serve hot.

Yields: 8 servings

Margaret Young

♦ GREEN BEANS ♦
SUPREME

2	10-ounce packages frozen French-cut green beans
2	tablespoons margarine or butter, melted
1/2	cup chopped onion
2	tablespoons all-purpose flour
	Salt and pepper
1	cup sour cream
1/2	cup shredded cheddar cheese

Preheat oven to 350 degrees. Cook the beans according to the package directions. Drain.

Saute the onions in margarine until tender. Add the flour, salt and pepper, mix well. Blend in the sour cream. Heat thoroughly, but do not boil. Add the green beans and stir. Pour the bean mixture into a 1 1/2-quart casserole. Top with cheese. Bake at 350 degrees for 15 minutes.

Yields: 6 to 8 servings

Deborah Alston

◆ GREEN BEANS ◆
WITH ALMONDS

1	pound green beans, French sliced
1/4	cup blanched slivered almonds
1	10 3/4-ounce can cream of mushroom soup
1/2	cup white wine

Presoak a clay pot, top and bottom, in water for 15 minutes. Place the beans in the presoaked pot, and top with the almonds. Combine the soup with white wine and add to the pot. Cover the pot and place it in a cold oven. Set the oven temperature at 450 degrees and bake for 1 hour.

Yields: 4 servings

Karen Harris

◆ Bow Ties with ◆ Bacon and Tomato Sauce

This pasta is delicious! It's easy to prepare and leftovers can easily be reheated.

7 to 8	slices bacon, diced
1	medium onion, finely chopped
2	14 1/2-ounce cans Italian pasta-style crushed tomatoes
1 1/2	teaspoons sugar
1	teaspoon salt
1/4	teaspoon pepper
1	16-ounce package bow tie or small shell macaroni
1/4	cup heavy or whipping cream
1	tablespoon chopped parsley

In a skillet over medium-low heat, cook the bacon until browned. With slotted spoon, remove the bacon to paper towels to drain. Pour off all but two tablespoons of bacon fat from skillet. In hot bacon fat, over medium heat, cook the onion until tender. Add the tomatoes with their liquid, sugar, salt, and pepper. Stir to break up the tomatoes. Over high heat, bring the mixture to a boil. Reduce heat to low; cover and simmer for 15 minutes.

Cook the macaroni according to the package directions, but do not add salt to the water. Drain. Stir the cream and parsley into the tomato mixture; heat through, but do not boil or mixture may curdle. To serve, place the pasta in a large deep platter and spoon the sauce over pasta. Sprinkle with bacon and toss.

Yields: 6 servings

Deborah Alston

◆ MACARONI & CHEESE ◆ DELUXE CASSEROLE

Rich and delicious.

1	8-ounce package macaroni
2	cups cottage cheese
1	8-ounce package sour cream
1	egg, beaten
3/4	teaspoon salt
	Pepper
2	cups (8 ounces) shredded sharp cheese
	Paprika

Preheat oven to 350 degrees. Cook and rinse the macaroni.

Combine the cottage cheese, sour cream, egg, salt, pepper, and sharp cheese. Mix the cottage cheese mixture with the cooked macaroni. Pour the macaroni in a 2-quart casserole and sprinkle with paprika.

Bake at 350 degrees for 45 minutes.

Yields: 4 to 6 servings

Eleanor Helms

◆MASHED POTATOES◆

Evaporated milk gives these
potatoes a special flavor.

2	pounds baking potatoes, peeled and sliced
1	onion, chopped
1 1/2	teaspoons salt
1/4	cup evaporated milk
1/4	cup water
4	tablespoons unsalted margarine or butter
1/8	teaspoon nutmeg (optional)
1/4	cup freshly grated Parmesan cheese (optional)

Place the potatoes and onions in a large saucepan with 1 teaspoon of salt. Add water to cover and bring to a boil over high heat. Reduce heat to medium and boil for 12 to 15 minutes, until potatoes are tender. Drain thoroughly, return the potatoes to the pan, and set aside for 5 minutes to let the water evaporate. Mash the potatoes and onions with an electric mixer.

Warm the milk in a medium saucepan over moderate heat. Add the butter and let it melt. Add the remaining 1/2 teaspoon salt. Pour the milk mixture over the potatoes, a little bit at a time, mixing constantly. Add the nutmeg and cheese and continue mixing until well blended and smooth. The potatoes may be kept warm for up to 1 hour in a 300 degree oven until ready to serve.

Variation: Leftover potatoes make excellent potato pancakes. Combine 2 cups potatoes, 1/2 cup onion (chopped and sauted), 1 egg and 2 tablespoons flour. Pat out potato pancakes and fry in non-stick frying pan.

Yields: 8 to 10 servings

Karen Harris

◆ SAVORY POTATOES ◆

1 1/2	cups water
1/2	teaspoon salt
2	tablespoons butter
1	tablespoons minced onion
1/2	cup milk
1 1/2	cups instant potato flakes
1/2	cup sour cream
1	egg, slightly beaten
	Chives
	Swiss cheese, grated

On high setting, microwave the water, salt, butter and minced onion for 3 to 4 minute, or until the mixture comes to a boil. Stir in the milk and potato flakes. Blend in the sour cream and egg.

Sprinkle the chives and grated Swiss cheese on top. Put the potatoes in a 1 1/2-quart vegetable dish. Microwave for 6 to 8 minutes. Let stand for 3 minutes before serving.

Yields: 5 servings

Eleanor Helms

◆ CHEDDARY MASHED ◆ POTATO AND CORN BAKE

3   cups water
2   tablespoons margarine
2 1/3   cups instant mashed potato flakes or buds
1   10 3/4-ounce can Campbell's golden corn soup
1/2   cup shredded Cheddar cheese
1/3   cup sour cream or plain yogurt
2   tablespoons chopped green onion
         Generous dash pepper

Heat the water and margarine to boiling. Stir to melt the margarine. Stir in the instant potatoes and stir until water is absorbed.

In a 1 1/2 quart casserole, combine the soup, Cheddar cheese, sour cream, onion and pepper. Mix in the potatoes until blended. Bake at 350 degrees for 30 minutes until hot and bubbling.

Yields: 8 servings

Pat Rush

◆ POTATO CASSEROLE ◆

6 to 8   large potatoes
1   8-ounce carton sour cream
1   stick margarine
2   tablespoons frozen chives
         Salt and pepper to taste
6 to 8   slices of bacon, cooked, drained and crumbled
1   cup grated sharp cheese

Preheat oven to 350 degrees. Boil and mash the potatoes; add the sour cream, margarine, chives, salt, pepper, and bacon. Pour into a 2-quart casserole dish sprayed with cooking spray. Sprinkle grated cheese on top of potatoes.

Bake at 350 degrees for 20 to 30 minutes.

Yields: 6 to 8 servings

Eleanor Helms

◆ ESCALLOPED POTATOES ◆

An old family favorite.

4	*large potatoes (4 cups), peeled and sliced*
2	*tablespoons all-purpose flour*
	Salt and pepper
	Grated nutmeg
2	*tablespoons finely minced fresh parsley*
4	*tablespoons margarine or butter*
1 1/4	*cups milk*
1/8	*teaspoon paprika*

Preheat oven to 325 degrees. Oil a rectangular baking dish and arrange some of the potato slices on the bottom. Sprinkle very lightly with flour. Add salt, pepper, and nutmeg to taste, then sprinkle on some of the parsley. Repeat, making 2 or 3 more layers.

Heat the margarine and milk together in a small saucepan over low heat; pour over the potatoes. Top with paprika. Bake covered at 325 degrees for 1 1/2 hours, or until a nice golden brown crust forms on top and the potatoes are tender.

Yields: 4 to 6 servings

Karen Harris

◆ RICE WITH ◆
MUSHROOMS

2	*tablespoons margarine or butter*
1/4	*cup finely chopped onion*
1/4	*pound fresh mushrooms, cut into small cubes*
	Salt, if desired
	Pepper to taste
1	*cup uncooked rice*
1 1/3	*cups fresh or canned chicken broth*

Heat 1 tablespoon margarine in a saucepan and add the onion. Cook, stirring occasionally, until tender. Add the mushrooms and cook about 3 minutes, stirring continuously. Add salt and pepper to taste. Add the rice and stir.

Add the broth and bring to a boil. Cover and simmer for 17 minutes. Remove from heat. Add the remaining margarine and fluff the rice with a fork.

Yields: 4 servings

Margaret Young

◆ CONSOMME RICE ◆

1/3   cup onion, chopped
1/2   stick margarine
1   cup rice, uncooked
3/4   teaspoon salt
1   tablespoon Worcestershire sauce
1   10 1/2-ounce can beef consomme
1   cup boiling water
1   beef bouillon cube
    Almonds, optional to garnish

Preheat oven to 350 degrees. Saute the onion in the margarine. Put the onion in the bottom of a casserole dish. Add the rice, salt and Worcestershire sauce to the casserole. Dissolve the bouillon cube in boiling water. Pour the bouillon and consomme over the rice mixture. Bake at 350 degrees about 30 minutes until the rice is done.

Jackie Brown

◆ PAT'S HOT RICE ◆

1/3   pound hot sausage
1   medium onion, chopped
1   cup regular rice, cooked according to directions
1/2   7-ounce jar chopped pimento
    Louisiana Hot Sauce

Brown the sausage in a skillet. Drain off the fat. Add the onion and saute with the sausage. Add the rice, pimento and hot sauce, to taste. Heat through.

Serves 4 to 6

Pat Rush

◆ Spinach Casserole ◆

2   packages frozen chopped spinach
1/2   teaspoon sugar
3/4   can cream of mushroom soup
8   ounces grated cheddar cheese
1   egg, beaten
        Bread crumbs or crushed crackers

Preheat oven to 350 degrees. Partially cook spinach in small amount of water with 1/2 teaspoon sugar added. Drain. Mix in the soup, cheese and beaten egg. Place in 1 1/2 quart buttered casserole. Top with crumbs or crackers. Bake at 350 degrees for 45 minutes.

Variation: Substitute broccoli for the spinach.

Yields: 6 to 8 servings

Eleanor Helms

♦ SQUASH CASSEROLE ♦

2	pounds squash, sliced
1	cup chopped onion
2	eggs
1	cup cracker crumbs
1	cup sharp cheddar cheese
2	tablespoons margarine
1	teaspoon salt
1/2	teaspoon black pepper

Preheat oven to 350 degrees. Cook the squash and onion in small amount of water until tender. Pour off the excess water and mash. Add the eggs, crumbs, cheese, margarine, salt and pepper. Mix well and pour into a casserole dish sprayed with cooking spray. Bake at 350 degrees for 35 to 45 minutes.

Yields: 6 to 8 servings

Pat Rush

♦ STRING BEANS ♦

1 1/2	pounds fresh string beans, in 1/4" pieces
	Stalk of celery, chopped
1/8 to 1/4	teaspoon dill seed
	Garlic salt to taste
1/4	cup chopped onion
	Sugar to taste
1/2	stick margarine

Combine the beans, celery, dill seed, garlic salt, onion, sugar and margarine in a pan with lid. Add water, cover and cook for 3 hours.

Ethel Weeks

♦ ORIENTAL PEA ♦ CASSEROLE

1   cup chopped celery
1   medium onion, chopped
1   green pepper, chopped
1   stick margarine
2   cups green peas
1   small jar pimentos
1   10 3/4-ounce can cream of celery soup
1   can sliced water chestnuts, adding liquid if needed

Preheat the oven to 350 degrees. Saute the celery, onion and pepper in the margarine. Stir in the peas, pimentos, celery soup and water chestnuts.

Pour into 1 1/2-quart casserole and bake at 350 degrees for 25 to 30 minutes.

Yields: 6 to 8 servings

Martha Helms

◆ SWEET POTATO ◆ CASSEROLE

4	medium-large sweet potatoes
1	stick margarine
1	cup sugar
2	cups brown sugar

Preheat oven to 350 degrees. Boil the sweet potatoes in water. Cook about 20 minutes, until tender. Peel, cut and slice into round pieces, about 3/4" thick to keep from falling apart, and place in a casserole dish.

In a small saucepan, mix the margarine, white sugar, and brown sugar over low heat until the margarine melts. Stir constantly to keep sugars from burning. Pour the syrup over potatoes. Bake uncovered at 350 degrees for 45 minutes, until the syrup is thick.

Yields: 6 servings

Ida Helms

◆ DELUXE SWEET ◆
POTATO CASSEROLE

Sweet potatoes:
3	cups sweet potatoes, cooked and mashed
2/3	cup sugar
1/2	cup condensed milk
1	teaspoon vanilla
1	stick margarine
1/2	teaspoon salt

Topping:
1/2	cup brown sugar
1/2	cup pecans
1	tablespoon all-purpose flour
1/4	stick of margarine
	Marshmallows

Preheat oven to 325 degrees.

To prepare the potatoes: Mix the potatoes, sugar, milk, vanilla, margarine and salt; pour into buttered dish. Bake at 325 degrees for 30 minutes.

To prepare the topping: Combine the brown sugar, pecans, flour and margarine; and pour on top of the casserole. Top with marshmallows. Return to the oven for 5 minutes or until the marshmallows are melted.

Yields: 4 servings

Jackie Brown

◆ STEWED TOMATO ◆
CASSEROLE

2	cans stewed tomatoes
1	teaspoon minced onion
1 to 2	teaspoons sugar
10 to 12	Ritz crackers, crumbled
1	tablespoon margarine, melted
	Salt and pepper to taste

Preheat oven to 350 degrees. Combine the stewed tomatoes, onion, sugar, crackers, margarine, salt and pepper. Pour into a casserole dish.

Bake at 350 degrees for 15 minutes.

Yields: 4 to 6 servings

Jackie Brown

♦ CAKES ♦

Charlie and Margaret Young
December, 1951

Paul and Gwen Allen
May, 1952

On August 23, 1951, Paul Allen passed away. Granny had her hands full with five children to raise and a family business to run. At the time, Granny's oldest child, Paul, was in Korea and her youngest child, Eleanor was only 12. She had many challenges ahead of her.

One of Pat's vivid memories of her father's funeral was watching his employees at the funeral home, crying. Her father had always taken care of his employees, making sure that their families were adequately cared for. Granny stepped into my grandfather's shoes and looked after these employees throughout her life. After she retired from the business, these folks became a part of our extended family. Over the years, she regularly collected clothes and food from family members and delivered them to her friends. I accompanied Granny on many of her visits; I can still picture their broad smiles when Granny appeared at their door. I realize now, that they loved her nearly as much as I did.

◆ POUND CAKE ◆

This is the best pound cake you will ever taste.

2	*sticks Fleischmann's margarine*
1/2	*cup Crisco shortening*
3	*cups sugar*
5	*eggs*
3	*cups all-purpose flour*
1/2	*teaspoon baking powder*
1/4	*teaspoon salt*
1	*cup milk*
1 1/2	*teaspoons vanilla*

Preheat oven to 325 degrees. Cream the margarine and shortening. Add the sugar and continue creaming until light and fluffy. Add the eggs one at a time, beating well after each egg.

Sift together the flour, baking powder and salt. Add alternately the dry ingredients and milk to the creamed mixture. Blend thoroughly. Add the vanilla. Scrape the sides of the bowl with a rubber spatula and beat for one minute.

Pour the batter into a greased and floured 10-inch tube pan. Bake at 325 degrees for 1 hour 10 minutes, until cake is golden brown and cooks away from the pan.

Yields: 12 to 16 servings

Eleanor Helms

◆ GERMAN CHOCOLATE ◆ POUND CAKE

3	cups sugar
2	sticks margarine
1/2	cup vegetable shortening
5	eggs
1	bar German chocolate, melted
3	cups all-purpose flour
1	teaspoon baking powder
1/2	teaspoon salt
1/2	teaspoon lemon extract
1 1/2	teaspoons vanilla
1	cup milk
1	cup nuts, optional
1	stick soft margarine
2	squares bitter chocolate, melted and cooled
1	teaspoon lemon juice
1	box powdered sugar, sifted
	Milk

Preheat oven to 300 degrees. Cream the sugar, margarine and shortening. Add the eggs one at a time, beating after each egg. Add the German chocolate. Sift the flour with the baking powder and salt. Add the flour to the margarine mixture, alternately with the milk. Add the vanilla and mix. Add the nuts. Pour the batter into a greased and floured 10-inch tube pan. Bake at 300 degrees for 1 1/2 hours.

Combine the soft margarine, bitter chocolate, lemon juice, and sugar. Add enough milk to adjust spreading consistency for icing. Ice the top and sides of the pound cake.

Yields: 12 to 16 servings

Margaret Young

♦ PINEAPPLE ♦
POUND CAKE

Cake:

1/2	cup vegetable shortening
2	sticks margarine
2 3/4	cups sugar
6	eggs
3	cups all-purpose flour
1	teaspoon baking powder
1/4	cup milk
1	teaspoon vanilla
1	small can crushed pineapple with syrup

Icing:

1/4	cup margarine
1 1/2	cups confectioners' sugar
1/4	cup drained pineapple

To prepare the cake: Using a mixer, combine the shortening, margarine and sugar. Add the eggs, one at a time, and beat. While beating, gradually add the flour. Add the baking powder, milk, and vanilla. Beat well. Fold in the pineapple.

Pour the batter into a greased and floured 10-inch tube pan. Do not preheat the oven. Starting with a *cold* oven, place pan in oven and bake at 325 degrees for 1 hour, 15 minutes.

To prepare the icing: Using a mixer, beat the margarine, sugar and pineapple. Ice the cooled cake.

Yields: 12 to 16 servings

Margaret Young

◆ LEMON JELLO ◆
POUND CAKE

Cake:

1	package lemon Jello
1	package yellow cake mix
3/4	cup water
1	teaspoon lemon flavoring
3/4	cup salad oil
4	eggs

Icing:

2	tablespoons margarine or butter
3	tablespoons milk
2	cups sifted confectioners' sugar
3	tablespoons lemon juice
1	teaspoon grated lemon rind

To prepare the cake: Preheat oven to 350 degrees. Add the dry Jello to the cake mix and stir. Add the water, lemon flavoring, oil and eggs. Using an electric mixer, beat the batter for 4 minutes at medium speed. Pour the batter into a greased and floured 10-inch tube pan. Bake at 350 degrees for 35 to 45 minutes, until golden. Let cool in pan 15 minutes.

To prepare the icing: Heat the milk and margarine. Add the milk mixture to the sugar. Add the lemon juice and lemon rind. Mix and spread on the cake.

Yields: 12 to 16 servings

Jackie Brown

♦ CREAM CHEESE ♦
POUND CAKE

2   sticks margarine or butter, softened
3   cups sugar
1   8-ounce package cream cheese, softened
6   eggs
3   cups all-purpose flour, sifted

Preheat oven to 325 degrees. Cream the margarine and sugar together. Add the cream cheese. Add the eggs and flour alternately, ending with flour. Using an electric mixer, beat the batter at medium speed for 3 minutes.

Pour the batter into a greased and floured 10-inch tube pan. Bake at 325 degrees for 1 hour, 20 minutes.

Yields: 12 to 16 servings

Betty Young

◆ GERMAN ◆
CHOCOLATE CAKE

A lot of work, but well worth the effort.

Cake:

1	package sweet German chocolate
1/2	cup boiling water
2	sticks margarine or butter
2	cups sugar
4	egg yokes, unbeaten
1	teaspoon vanilla
2 1/2	cups cake flour, sifted
1	teaspoon baking soda
1/2	teaspoon salt
1	cup buttermilk
4	egg whites, beaten stiff

Icing:

1	cup evaporated milk
1	cup sugar
3	egg yokes
2	sticks margarine or butter
1	teaspoon vanilla
1	cup pecans chopped
1	small can angel flake coconut

To prepare the cake: Preheat the oven to 350 degrees. Melt the chocolate in the boiling water and let cool. Cream the margarine and sugar until light. Add the egg yokes one at time, beating after each. Add the vanilla and chocolate. Mix until blended.

Sift together the flour, baking soda, and salt. Add the flour mixture to the margarine mixture, alternately with milk, beating after each addition. Fold in the egg whites. Pour into three greased and floured round cake pans. Bake at 350 degrees for 35-40 minutes. Let the cake cool before icing.

To prepare the icing: In a saucepan, combine the evaporated milk, sugar, egg yokes, margarine, and vanilla. Cook the icing for 12 minutes at medium heat, or until thick. Add the pecans and coconut. Beat until cool and spreadable. Frost between the cake layers and top, but not the cake sides.

Yields: 12 to 16 servings

Margaret Young

◆ WATT'S FAVORITE ◆
CARAMEL CAKE

Cake:

2	sticks margarine
2	cups sugar
2	egg yokes
2	whole eggs
1	cup buttermilk
3/4	teaspoon baking soda
2 1/2	cups all-purpose flour, sifted
1	teaspoon vanilla

Caramel Icing:

4	cups (1 1/2 boxes) brown sugar
1/2	cup plus 2 tablespoons light whipping cream
2	sticks margarine
1	teaspoon vanilla
1	teaspoon baking powder

To prepare the cake: Preheat oven to 350 degrees. Combine the margarine, sugar, egg yolks, eggs, buttermilk, baking soda, flour and vanilla. Mix well.

Pour batter into three greased round cake pans. Bake at 350 degrees for 25 to 30 minutes.

To prepare the icing: Mix the brown sugar, whipping cream and margarine and bring to a boil over medium heat. Boil for 2 minutes. Add the vanilla and baking powder. Beat with hand mixer until icing can spread.

Yields: 10 to 12 servings

Margaret Young

♦ CHOCOLATE CAKE ♦

1	stick margarine or butter
2 1/2	squares unsweetened chocolate
2	cups sugar
1	cup water
2	cups all-purpose flour
1	teaspoon salt
1	teaspoon baking powder
2	eggs
1/2	cup buttermilk*
1	teaspoon baking soda
1	teaspoon vanilla

Preheat oven to 350 degrees. Melt and cool the margarine and chocolate. Add the sugar and water. Add the flour, salt, baking powder and mix. Add the eggs one at a time and beat well after each egg. Add the buttermilk, baking soda, vanilla. Mix well.

Pour the batter into a greased sheet cake pan. Bake at 350 degrees for 30 minutes.

*Variation: Substitute 1/2 cup milk and 1/2 tablespoon vinegar for the buttermilk.

Yields: 10 to 12 servings

Eleanor Helms

♦ PAT'S CHOCOLATE ♦ FUDGE CAKE

Cake:

1   egg
1/4   cup sugar
1   8-ounce package of cream cheese, softened
3   tablespoons milk
2   tablespoons margarine or butter, softened
1   tablespoon cornstarch
1/2   teaspoon vanilla extract
4   1-ounce squares unsweetened chocolate
1   stick margarine or butter, softened
2   cups sugar
2   eggs
2   cups all-purpose flour
1   teaspoon baking powder
1/2   teaspoon baking soda
1/4   teaspoon salt
1 1/3 cups milk
1   teaspoon vanilla extract

Frosting:

2   1-ounce squares unsweetened chocolate
1/4   cup margarine or butter
3 1/2 cups sifted powdered sugar
1/3   cup milk
1   teaspoon vanilla extract

To prepare the cake: Preheat oven to 350 degrees. Combine one egg, 1/4 cup sugar and cream cheese in a medium mixing bowl. Beat mixture at high speed with an electric blender until smooth. Gradually add 3 tablespoons milk, 2 tablespoons margarine, cornstarch, and 1/2 teaspoon vanilla extract. Beat well and set aside.

Place the 4 chocolate squares in the top of a double boiler. Bring the water to a boil and reduce the heat to low. Heat until the chocolate melts, stirring occasionally. Remove from heat and let cool.

Cream 1 stick margarine and gradually add 2 cups sugar. Beat well at medium speed. Add two eggs, one at a time, beating well after each addition. Combine the flour, baking powder, baking soda and salt and stir well. Add the flour mixture to creamed mixture alternately with 1 1/3 cups milk, beginning and ending with flour mixture. Mix after each addition. Stir in the melted chocolate and vanilla extract. Spread half of this chocolate batter into a greased and floured 13x9-inch baking pan. Spoon reserved cream cheese mixture evenly over the batter. Top with the remaining half of chocolate batter. Bake at 350 degrees for 55 to 60 minutes until a wooden tooth pick inserted in center comes out clean. Let cool completely in pan on a wire rack.

To prepare the frosting: Combine chocolate and margarine in the top of a double boiler. Bring water to a boil. Reduce heat to low and heat until chocolate and margarine melt, stirring occasionally. Remove mixture from heat and let cool. Add powdered sugar and milk to chocolate mixture, beating at medium speed with an electric mixer until smooth. Stir in the vanilla. Frost the cooled cake.

Yields: 10 to 12 servings

Pat Rush

♦ ELEANOR'S CHOCOLATE ♦ FUDGE CAKE

Cake:
1/2	cup margarine or butter, softened
1	16-ounce package brown sugar
3	eggs
3	1-ounce squares unsweetened chocolate, melted
2 1/4	cups sifted cake flour
1/2	teaspoon salt
2	teaspoons baking soda
1	cup sour cream
1	cup hot water
1 1/2	teaspoons vanilla extract

Frosting:
3	1-ounce squares unsweetened chocolate
1/2	cup margarine or butter
1	16-ounce package powdered sugar, sifted
1/3	cup milk
2	teaspoons vanilla extract

To prepare the cake: Cream the margarine. Gradually add the brown sugar, beating well. Add the eggs, one at a time, beating well after each addition. Add the chocolate, mixing well.

Combine the flour, salt and baking soda. Gradually add the flour to the chocolate mixture alternately with sour cream, beating well after each addition. Add water, mixing well. Stir in the vanilla extract. The batter will be thin.

Pour the batter evenly into two greased and floured 9-inch cake pans. Bake at 350 degrees for 45 minutes or until cake tests done. Let cool in pans 10 minutes; remove layers from pans, and place on wire racks to complete cooling.

To prepare the frosting: Combine the chocolate and margarine over low heat until melted, stirring constantly. Combine the sugar, milk, and vanilla in a medium mixing bowl; mix well. Set the bowl in a large pan of ice water, and stir in chocolate mixture; beat approximately 2 minutes at high speed with an electric mixer until the mixture is the appropriate spreading consistency.

Yields: 10 to 12 servings

Eleanor Helms

♦ SOUR CREAM ♦ FUDGE CAKE

2	*cups sifted cake flour*
1 1/2	*cups sugar*
1	*teaspoon baking soda*
1	*teaspoon salt*
1/2	*cup vegetable shortening*
1	*cup sour cream*
3	*1-ounce squares unsweetened chocolate, melted*
2	*eggs*
1	*teaspoon vanilla*
1/4	*cup hot water*

Preheat the oven to 350 degrees. Sift together the flour, sugar, baking soda, and salt. Add the shortening and sour cream. With electric mixer, blend for two minutes, initially at low speed and then at medium speed. Add the chocolate, eggs, vanilla and water and beat for two minutes.

Pour the batter into two 8-inch pans well greased and lightly floured on the bottoms. Bake at 350 degrees for 30 to 35 minutes. Cool and frost with your favorite fudge frosting.

Yields: 10 to 12 servings

Margaret Young

♦ CHOCOLATE ♦
ECLAIR CAKE

Cake:
1   box graham crackers
2   small packages vanilla instant pudding
1   8-ounce carton of Cool Whip topping
2 3/4 cups milk

Frosting:
2   1-ounce packets unsweetened chocolate Nestle Choco-Bake
1 1/2 cups confectioners' sugar
2   teaspoons vanilla
3   tablespoons margarine, at room temperature
2   tablespoons light corn syrup

To prepare the cake: Line the bottom of a 9x13-inch baking pan with graham crackers. Combine the pudding mix, 2/3 cup of milk and Cool Whip. Beat well. Pour half of mix over the crackers. Place a layer of graham crackers, the remaining pudding mix and another layer of graham crackers.

To prepare frosting: Mix the Choco-Bake, sugar, vanilla, margarine and corn syrup. Beat until creamy. Spread over the cracker layer and refrigerate overnight.

Yields: 10 to 12 servings

Pat Rush

◆ WHITE ◆
CHOCOLATE CAKE

Cake:

1/4	pound white chocolate
1/2	cup boiling water
2	sticks margarine or butter
2	cups sugar
4	egg yolks
1	teaspoon vanilla
2 1/2	cups cake flour
1	teaspoon baking soda
1	cup buttermilk
4	egg whites
1	cup chopped pecans
1	cup flaked coconut

Frosting:

1	cup evaporated milk
1	cup sugar
3	egg yokes
1	stick margarine or butter
1	teaspoon vanilla
1 1/3	cups coconut
1	cup chopped pecans

To prepare the cake: Preheat the oven to 350 degrees. Melt the chocolate in the boiling water and set aside to cool.

Cream the margarine and sugar until fluffy. Mix in the egg yolks one at a time, beating well after each addition. Add the melted chocolate and vanilla. Sift together the flour and baking soda and add to the creamed mixture. Add the buttermilk and just slightly blend. (Do not over mix at this point). Beat the egg whites until stiff and fold in. Slightly blend. Gently stir in pecans and coconut.

Pour the batter into three greased and floured 9-inch pans. Bake in a 350 degree oven for 30 minutes or until the cake tests done.

To prepare the frosting: Combine the milk, sugar, egg yolks, margarine and vanilla in saucepan. Cook over medium heat, stirring constantly until mixture thickens, about 12 minutes.

Remove from the heat. Add the coconut and pecans. Beat and spread on cake.

Yields: 10 to 12 servings

Margaret Young

◆ ITALIAN CREAM CAKE ◆

Cake:

2	cups sugar
1	stick margarine or butter, softened
1/2	cup shortening
5	eggs, separated
1	teaspoon baking soda
1	cup buttermilk
2	cups all-purpose flour, sifted
1	cup angel flaked coconut
1	teaspoon vanilla

Frosting:

1	8-ounce package cream cheese, softened
1	stick margarine or butter, soft
1	box confectioners' sugar, sifted
1 1/2	teaspoons vanilla
1	cup pecans, chopped
	Milk to moisten

To prepare the cake: Preheat the oven to 350 degrees. Cream the sugar, margarine and shortening. Add the egg yolks, beating after each addition. Dissolve the baking soda in the buttermilk and add alternately with flour to egg mixture. Add the coconut. Beat the egg whites until stiff and fold in. Add the vanilla. Pour into three 8-inch greased and floured cake pans. Bake at 350 degrees for 25 to 30 minutes. Cool the cakes.

To prepare the frosting: Mix the margarine and cream cheese. Add the sugar, vanilla and nuts. Moisten the frosting with milk, if needed, to spreading consistency. Frost the tops and sides of layers.

Yields: 12 to 16 servings

Margaret Young

◆ MISSISSIPPI ◆ MUD CAKE

Cake:
2	sticks margarine
2	cups sugar
1/3	cup cocoa
1 1/2	cups self-rising flour
1	can coconut
1	cup pecans
4	eggs, beaten

Frosting:
7	ounces marshmallow creme
3/4	stick margarine, melted
1/3	cup cocoa
1/4	cup milk
1/2	box confectioners' sugar
1	teaspoon vanilla

To prepare the cake: Preheat oven to 350 degrees. Melt the margarine. In a bowl, combine the sugar, cocoa, flour, coconut, pecans and eggs. Pour margarine in the bowl. Mix well. Pour the batter in a greased, floured 9x13x2-inch pan and bake at 350 degrees for 40 minutes or until done.

To prepare frosting: Spread the marshmallow creme over cake while cake is still hot. Mix the margarine, cocoa, milk, sugar and vanilla and spread mixture over the creme. Swirl.

Yields: 12 to 16 servings

Mary Calhoun

◆ PINEAPPLE ◆
ICE BOX CAKE

The Allen children grew up with this dessert.

1	stick margarine
3/4	cup sugar
1	large egg, well beaten
3/4	cup chopped pecans
1	large can of pineapple, well drained
1	box vanilla wafers
	Whipped cream

Cream the margarine and sugar until fluffy. Add the egg and mix well. Add the nuts and pineapple and stir.

Crumb the vanilla wafers in a food processor. Evenly distribute one-half of the wafer crumbs in a 9x13-inch pan. Spread the pineapple mixture over the crumbs. Add remaining crumbs.

Refrigerate the cake for a minimum of four hours. Serve with whipped cream.

Yields: 12 servings

Gladys Allen

♦ APPLE PECAN CAKE ♦

Cake:
3	eggs beaten
2	cups sugar
1/2	cup vegetable oil
2	teaspoons vanilla
2	cups all-purpose flour
2	teaspoons baking soda
2	teaspoons cinnamon
1/2	teaspoon nutmeg
1/4	teaspoon salt
4	cups diced unpeeled apples
1	cup chopped pecans

Frosting:
2	3 ounce packages cream cheese, softened
1/2	stick margarine
1 1/2	cups confectioners' sugar
1/2	teaspoon vanilla

To prepare the cake: Preheat the oven to 325 degrees. In a large mixing bowl, beat together the eggs, sugar, oil and vanilla. Combine the flour, baking soda, cinnamon, nutmeg and salt. Add the dry ingredients to the batter. Fold in the apples and nuts. Spread the batter into 13x9x2-inch greased and floured baking pan. Bake at 325 degrees for 1 hour or until the cake tests done. Cool.

To prepare the frosting: Combine the cream cheese, margarine, sugar and vanilla. Whip until smooth and spread over the cake.

Yields: 10 to 12 servings

Pat Rush

◆ SPICE LAYER CAKE ◆

Cake:

3/4	cup vegetable shortening
2 1/4	cups cake flour, sifted
1	cup sugar
1	teaspoon baking powder
1	teaspoon salt
3/4	teaspoon baking soda
3/4 to 1	teaspoon cinnamon
3/4 to 1	teaspoon ground cloves
3/4	cup brown sugar
1	cup buttermilk
3	eggs, slightly beaten

Frosting:

2	egg whites
3/4	cup granulated sugar
3/4	cup brown sugar
1 1/2	teaspoons corn syrup
1/3	cup cold water
	Dash salt
1	teaspoon vanilla
1/2	cup broken California walnuts

To prepare the cake: Preheat the oven to 350 degrees. Stir the shortening just to soften. Sift in the flour, sugar, salt, baking soda, and spices. Add the brown sugar and buttermilk. Mix until all of the flour is dampened. Then beat vigorously for 2 minutes. Add the eggs and beat 2 minutes longer. Bake in two paper-lined 9-inch round cake pans at 350 degrees for 20 to 35 minutes.

To prepare the frosting: In the top of a double boiler, place the egg whites, sugar, brown sugar, corn syrup, water, and a dash of salt. Continuously beat the mixture and cook for 7 minutes, until frosting holds peaks. Remove the icing from the heat and add the vanilla and nuts. Beat until the frosting spreads easily.

Yields: 12 to 16 servings

Margaret Young

◆ TOMATO SOUP ◆
SPICE CAKE

Cake:

1/2	cup vegetable shortening
1 1/2	cups sugar
2	eggs
2	cups sifted cake flour
2	teaspoons baking powder
1/4	teaspoon baking soda
1/2	teaspoon cinnamon
1/2	teaspoon ground cloves
1/2	teaspoon nutmeg
1	can condensed tomato soup
1	cup chopped nuts
1	cup seedless raisins

Frosting:

1	3-ounce package cream cheese, softened
1/2	teaspoon vanilla
2 1/2	cups sifted confectioners' sugar
2	teaspoons milk (approximately)

To prepare the cake: Preheat oven to 375 degrees. Stir the shortening to soften. Gradually add the sugar, creaming until light and fluffy. Add the eggs, one at a time, beating well after each addition. Sift together flour, baking powder, baking soda, cinnamon, cloves, and nutmeg. Add the flour to the creamed mixture alternately with soup, beginning and ending with the flour mixture, and beating well after each addition. Beat 1 minute longer; fold in nuts and raisins.

Pour the batter into two paper-lined 8-inch round pans at 375 degrees for 30 minutes or until done. Cool for 10 minutes and remove from pans.

To prepare the icing: Blend the cream cheese and vanilla. Gradually add the sugar, creaming well. Add enough milk to bring to spreading consistency. Frost the cake and border the top of the cake with white raisins and broken nuts.

Yields: 12 to 16 servings

Margaret Young

◆ CARROT CAKE ◆ WITH CREAM CHEESE FROSTING

Cake:

1 1/2	cups oil
2	cups sugar
4	eggs, well beaten
2	cups all-purpose flour
1	teaspoon salt, optional
2	teaspoons cinnamon
2	teaspoons baking soda
2	teaspoons baking powder
1	cup broken pecans
3	cups grated carrots

Frosting:

1/2 to 1	stick margarine, at room temperature
1	8-ounce package cream cheese, at room temperature
1	box confectioners' sugar
2	teaspoons vanilla

To prepare the cake: Mix the oil and sugar and beat well. Add the eggs and blend. Sift the flour, salt, cinnamon, baking soda, and baking powder two or three times. Add the nuts to the dry ingredients and blend thoroughly with other mixture. Add the carrots, small amounts at a time, and blend well.

Pour the batter into three paper-lined 8-inch layer cake pans and bake at 350 degrees for 30 minutes.

To prepare the frosting: Mix the margarine, cream cheese, confectioners' sugar and vanilla and blend until smooth and creamy. Spread the icing between the cake layers, and on the top and sides of the cake.

Yields: 12 to 16 servings

Margaret Young

♦ JIFFY ONE EGG CAKE ♦

*Easy to make layer cake, good
with fresh fruit and ice cream.*

1 1/2	cups all-purpose flour, sifted
3/4	cup granulated sugar
2	teaspoons baking powder
1/2	teaspoon salt
1/4	cup vegetable shortening
1/2	cup milk
1	egg, slightly beaten
1	teaspoon vanilla

Preheat oven to 350 degrees. Sift the dry ingredients, and add the shortening, milk, egg and flavoring. Beat about 2 1/2 minutes. Pour the batter into an 8-inch square pan and bake at 350 degrees for 25 minutes.

Yields: 6 to 8 servings

Margaret Young

◆ FESTIVE CAKE ◆

Cake:

3	cups all-purpose flour
2	cups sugar
1	teaspoon baking soda
1	teaspoon salt
1	teaspoon cinnamon
1	cup chopped almonds
3	eggs
1 1/2	cups vegetable oil
1	teaspoon almond extract
2	cups chopped firm, ripe bananas
1	8-ounce can crushed pineapple

Frosting:

1	8-ounce package of cream cheese, at room temperature
1	stick margarine or butter, at room temperature
1	box confectioners' sugar
1	tablespoon vanilla

To prepare the cake: Preheat oven to 325 degrees. Mix and sift the flour, sugar, baking soda, salt and cinnamon. Stir in the almonds. In a small bowl, beat the eggs slightly and add the oil, almond extract, bananas and undrained pineapple. Add the egg mixture to the dry ingredients. Mix thoroughly, but do not beat. Spoon into a well-oiled 10-inch tube pan. Bake at 325 degrees for 1 hour and 20 to 25 minutes. Remove the cake from the oven and let stand 10 to 15 minutes. Invert cake on wire rack and remove the pan. Cool thoroughly before frosting.

To prepare the frosting: Cream together the cream cheese and margarine. Add the sugar and vanilla. Frost top and sides. Store the cake in the refrigerator until ready to serve.

Margaret Young

◆ MARGARET'S ◆
ORANGE CAKE

A real family favorite!

Cake:

2 1/8	cups all-purpose flour, sifted
1 1/2	cups sugar
3	teaspoons baking powder
1	teaspoon salt
2/3	cup vegetable shortening
1	cup milk
1 1/2	teaspoons vanilla
3	eggs

Frosting:

1/3	stick margarine, melted
2	tablespoons milk
1	box confectioners' sugar
4	ounces concentrated frozen orange juice
2	tablespoons orange zest
1 1/2	tablespoons vegetable shortening

To prepare the cake: Preheat oven to 350 degrees. Sift together the flour, sugar, baking powder and salt. Add the shortening and mix well. Add half of the milk and the vanilla and beat for two minutes. Add the remaining milk and eggs and beat for two minutes. Pour the batter into two 9-inch greased and floured cake pans. Bake at 350 degrees for 30 to 35 minutes.

To prepare the frosting: Add one tablespoon milk to the melted margarine. Add half of the sugar and beat. Add the orange juice and orange zest and beat. Add the remaining sugar and beat. Add the shortening and beat. Add remaining milk, if needed, to bring to spreading consistency.

Margaret Young

◆ BANANA SOUR ◆ CREAM CAKE

1/2   cup chopped pecans
1/4   cup sugar
1/2   teaspoon ground cinnamon
1/2   cup shortening
1   cup sugar
2   eggs
1   cup mashed bananas
1   teaspoon vanilla extract
1/2   cup sour cream
2   cups all-purpose flour
1   teaspoon baking powder
1   teaspoon baking soda
1/4   teaspoon salt

Preheat oven to 350 degrees. Combine the pecans, 1/4 cup sugar, and cinnamon, stir well and set aside.

Combine the shortening and sugar. Cream until light and fluffy. Beat in the eggs, bananas, and vanilla. Stir in the sour cream. Sift the flour, baking powder, baking soda and salt and add to creamed mixture. Stir just enough to blend.

Sprinkle 1/4 of cinnamon mixture into bottom of a well-greased 10-inch bundt pan. Spoon half of the batter into the pan. Sprinkle the remaining cinnamon-nut mixture over the batter and spoon the remaining batter into the pan. Bake at 350 degrees 40 to 50 minutes or until the cake tests done. Cool the cake for 5 minutes in the pan. Remove and cool on wire rack.

Yields: 10 to 12 servings

Margaret Young

◆ PINEAPPLE ◆
UPSIDE-DOWN CAKE

2	tablespoons margarine or butter
1/2	cup brown sugar
4	canned pineapple slices, halved
4	maraschino cherries, halved
1/3	cup vegetable shortening
1 1/4	cups all-purpose flour
1/2	cup sugar
2	teaspoons baking powder
1/2	teaspoon salt
1/2	cup pineapple syrup
1/2	teaspoon grated lemon peel
1	egg

Preheat oven to 350 degrees. Melt the margarine in an 8-inch square pan. Stir in brown sugar. Arrange pineapple in mixture, placing a cherry half in each hollow.

In a bowl, stir shortening to soften. Sift in the flour, sugar, baking powder and salt. Add the syrup, lemon peel, and egg. Mix until all flour is dampened. Beat vigorously for 2 minutes. Pour the batter over pineapple.

Bake at 350 degrees for 30 to 35 minutes. Let the cake stand for 10 minutes. Invert the cake on a plate and serve warm with whipped cream.

Yields: 6 to 8 servings

Margaret Young

◆ PINEAPPLE ◆
CHIFFON CAKE

2 1/4   cups cake flour, sifted
1 1/2   cups sugar
3   teaspoons baking powder
1   teaspoon salt
1/2   cup salad oil
5   egg yolks
3/4   cup unsweetened pineapple juice
8   egg whites
1/2   teaspoon cream of tartar

Preheat oven to 325 degrees. Sift the dry ingredients into a mixing bowl. Make a well in the dry ingredients. In the following order, add the salad oil, egg yolks, and pineapple juice. Beat the batter until satin smooth.

In a large mixing bowl, combine the egg whites and cream of tartar; beat to very stiff peaks. Pour the egg-yolk batter in thin stream over entire surface of whites, gently cutting and folding just to blend.

Pour the batter into an ungreased 10-inch tube pan and bake at 325 degrees for 55 minutes. Increase the oven temperature to 350 degrees and bake for 10 minutes. Invert the pan and let the cake cool.

Yields: 10 to 12 servings

Margaret Young

◆ EASY BLUEBERRY ◆ DUMP CAKE

1   white cake mix
1   pint sweetened blueberries
1   can (15-16 ounce) crushed pineapple
1/2   cup broken pecans
1 1/2 sticks margarine or butter, melted

Put the berries in a 6x11-inch greased baking dish. Cover with pineapple. Pour on dry cake mix and scatter nuts over top. Drizzle margarine over the nuts. Bake for 1 hour at 350 degrees.

Serve the cake topped with ice cream or whipped cream.

Yields: 8 to 10 servings

Kathy Eudy

◆ BUTTERSCOTCH CAKE ◆

Cake:

2/3	cup butterscotch morsels
1/4	cup water
1/2	cup vegetable shortening
1 1/4	cups sugar
3	eggs
2 1/4	cups all-purpose flour
1/2	teaspoon baking powder
1	teaspoon baking soda
1/2	teaspoon salt
1	cup buttermilk

Butterscotch Filling:

1/2	cup sugar
1	tablespoon cornstarch
1/2	cup evaporated milk
1/3	cup water
1/3	cup butterscotch morsels
1	egg yolk, slightly beaten
2	tablespoons margarine or butter
1	cup chopped pecans
1	cup flaked coconut, chopped

Frosting:

1/3	cup sugar
1/3	cup firmly packed brown sugar
1/3	cup water
1	tablespoon corn syrup
1	egg white
1/4	teaspoon cream of tartar

To prepare the cake: Preheat oven to 375 degrees. Combine the butterscotch morsels and water in a small saucepan and place over low heat. Stir until melted and set aside to cool. Beat the shortening in a mixing bowl at medium speed with an electric mixer; gradually add the sugar, beating well. Add the eggs, one at a time, beating well after each addition. Add the butterscotch mixture. Combine the flour, baking powder, baking soda, and salt. Add the dry ingredients to the creamed mixture alternately with the buttermilk, beginning and ending with flour mixture.

Pour batter into two greased and floured 9-inch cake pans. Bake at 375 degrees for 25 to 30 minutes or until a wooden pick inserted in center comes out clean. Cool in the pans for 10 minutes. Remove the cakes from the pans and cool on wire racks.

To prepare the filling: Combine the sugar and cornstarch in a 2-quart saucepan. Stir in the milk and water. Add the butterscotch morsels and egg yolk. Stir well. Cook over medium heat, stirring constantly until smooth and thickened. Remove from the heat and stir in the margarine, pecans and coconut. Let cool.

To prepare the frosting: Combine the sugar, brown sugar, water and corn syrup. Cook over medium heat, stirring constantly until mixture is clear. Cook without stirring until mixture reaches soft ball stage (240 degrees). Combine the egg white and cream of tartar in a small mixing bowl. Beat at high speed with an electric mixture until soft peaks form. Continue to beat, slowly adding hot syrup in a steady stream. Beat constantly until mixture reaches spreading consistency.

Place a cake layer on a cake platter. Spread one cup of butterscotch filling on top of cake. Place the second layer on top of the filling. Spread the butterscotch filling to within 1/2 inch of edge on top of cake. Frost sides and top edge of cake with the frosting.

Yields: 12 to 16 servings

Margaret Young

♦ FIVE DAY ♦
COCONUT CAKE

2	cups sugar
18	ounces frozen coconut, thawed
16	ounce carton sour cream
1	white cake mix
1	carton Cool Whip

First day: Combine the sugar and 1 1/2 cups of coconut with the sour cream. Place sour cream mixture in a container with a tight fitting lid and refrigerate 24 hours, along with reserved coconut.

Second day: Bake the cake mix according to directions and cool thoroughly. Slice each layer in half horizontally, making four layers. Use the coconut mixture to ice between layers and on top. Refrigerate the cake in a tight-fitting container.

Fourth day: Ice the top and sides of the cake with the Cool Whip and sprinkle remaining coconut on top and sides. Refrigerate the cake and serve on the fifth day.

Yields: 8 to 10 servings

Jackie Brown

♦ COCONUT CAKE ♦

Cake:

1 1/2	cups butter-flavored Crisco
2 1/2	cups all-purpose flour
3	cups sugar
1	teaspoon baking powder
1/2	teaspoon salt
1	cup milk
5	eggs
1	cup frozen flaked coconut
2	teaspoons coconut flavoring

Frosting:

1	cup sugar
1/2	stick margarine or butter
2	tablespoons white Kayro syrup
1/2	cup buttermilk

To prepare the cake: Preheat oven to 300 degrees. Stir the Crisco in a bowl to soften. Sift together the flour, sugar, baking powder, and salt and add to the Crisco. Stir well. Add the milk and mix well. Add eggs, stirring after each addition. Fold in the coconut and coconut flavoring. Pour the batter into two 8-inch greased cake pans. Bake at 300 degrees for 1 1/2 hours.

To prepare the frosting: Place the sugar, margarine, syrup and buttermilk in a saucepan. Over medium-high heat, stir the syrup mixture continuously and bring to a boil for 4 to 5 minutes.

While the cake is warm, poke holes in the cake with a fork. Pour glaze over the cake. Let the cake cool for approximately one hour until totally cool.

Yields: 10 to 12 servings

Eleanor Helms

♦ COCONUT FRUITCAKE ♦

2   cups all-purpose flour
1   teaspoon baking powder
1   teaspoon salt
1   pound fruitcake mix
1 1/2 cups flaked coconut
1   cup golden raisins
1   cup chopped nuts
1   stick margarine
1   cup sugar
3   eggs, beaten
1   teaspoon lemon extract
1/2   cup orange juice

Preheat oven to 250 degrees. In a large bowl, combine the flour, baking powder, and salt. Add the fruitcake mix, coconut, raisins and nuts. Mix well.

In a mixing bowl, cream the margarine and sugar. Add the eggs and lemon extract. Mix well. Stir in the flour mixture, alternately with the orange juice. Pour into a greased 10-inch tube pan lined with waxed paper. Bake at 250 degrees for 2 to 2 1/2 hours or until cake tests done. Cool 10 minutes. Loosen edges with sharp knife. Remove from pan and cool completely on wire rack.

Yields: 12 to 16 servings

Pat Rush

◆ BUTTER FLUFF ◆ FRUIT DESSERT

1	round angel food cake
1	quart strawberries
1 1/2	sticks margarine or butter
1 1/2	cups sifted confectioners' sugar
1	teaspoon vanilla
4	egg whites
1 1/2	cups sifted confectioners' sugar

Using wooden picks for markers, cut cake into 3 layers. Set aside enough whole strawberries for garnish; slice remainder.

In a bowl, cream the margarine. Gradually add 1 1/2 cups confectioners' sugar. Beat until light and fluffy. Blend in the vanilla. Beat the egg whites until peaks fold over. Gradually add remaining confectioners' sugar. Beat until stiff peaks form. Using low speed of mixer, blend the creamed mixture into the egg white mixture carefully and do not over beat.

Place the bottom layer of cake on a serving plate and spread a layer of the frosting on the cut side. Cover with single layer of a sliced strawberries and another layer of frosting. Add the second layer of cake and fill as for first layer. Top with third layer of cake. Frost sides and top with remaining frosting. Garnish top with strawberry halves. Refrigerate until ready to serve. This cake will be at its best if served within a few hours after assembling.

Variations: Substitute raspberries, blueberries, or bing cherries for the strawberries.

Yields: 12 to 16 servings

Margaret Young

◆ Lemon Sponge Cake ◆

Cake:

1 1/4	cups cake flour, sifted
1	cup sugar
1/2	teaspoon double-acting baking powder
6	egg whites
1	teaspoon cream of tartar
1/2	teaspoon salt
1/2	cup sugar
6	egg yolks
1/4	cup cold water
1	teaspoon vanilla
1	teaspoon lemon extract.

Lemon Filling:

1	cup sugar
1/4	cup cornstarch
1/8	teaspoon salt
1 1/2	cups water
2	egg yolks, slightly beaten
2 to 3	teaspoons grated lemon rind
1/4	cup lemon juice
2	tablespoons margarine

To prepare the cake: Preheat oven to 350 degrees. Sift the flour, sugar and baking powder and set aside.

In medium mixing bowl, beat the egg whites, cream of tartar, and salt. Add sugar, one tablespoon at a time. Continue beating until very stiff with straight peaks forming. Do not under beat.

In a separate bowl, combine the egg yolks, water, vanilla, and lemon extract. Add the egg yolk mixture to flour mixture all at once. With an electric mixer, beat for 1 minute on medium speed.

Fold the batter, 1/4 at a time, into the beaten egg whites using a wire whip or spatula. Blend gently but thoroughly after each addition. Pour the batter into an ungreased 10-inch tube pan.

Bake at 350 degrees for 40 to 50 minutes. Invert immediately and cool in pan.

To prepare the lemon filling: Combine the sugar, cornstarch and salt in a saucepan. Add water and mix well. Cook over medium heat, stirring constantly, until thick and clear. Blend in the egg yolks to which a little of the hot mixture has been added. Cook 2 minutes, stirring constantly. Remove from heat. Stir in grated lemon rind, lemon juice and margarine. Cool thoroughly.

Cut cake into 8 layers. Spread Lemon Filling between layers. Frost top and sides with sour cream frosting.

Yields: 10 to 12 servings

Margaret Young

♦ LEMON JELLO CAKE ♦

Cake:

1	yellow cake mix
1	package lemon Jello
1	teaspoon lemon flavoring
3/4	cup water
3/4	cup salad oil
4	eggs

Glaze:

2	tablespoons milk
2	tablespoons margarine or butter, melted
2	cups sifted confectioners' sugar
3	tablespoons lemon juice
1	teaspoon grated lemon rind

To prepare the cake: Preheat the oven to 350 degrees. Mix the cake mix and Jello. Add the flavoring, water, salad oil and eggs. Beat for 4 minutes medium speed. Pour the batter into a 10-inch greased tube pan. Bake at 350 degrees for 45 minutes.

To prepare the glaze: Combine the milk, margarine, sugar, lemon juice and lemon rind. Beat with mixer. Spread on cake.

Yields: 12 to 14 servings

Margaret Young

◆ STRAWBERRY ROLL ◆

5	egg whites
1	cup sugar
5	egg yokes, beaten
	Juice and rind of 1 lemon
1	cup all-purpose flour, sifted
2	tablespoons sugar
1	quart of fresh strawberries
1/4	cup sugar
1	pint carton of whipping cream

Preheat oven to 350 degrees. On high speed of electric mixer, beat the egg whites until soft peaks form. Gradually add 1 cup of sugar. Turn mixer to low speed and quickly add the beaten egg yokes, lemon juice and rind. By hand, fold in flour, then pour into a jelly roll pan that has been greased and lined with paper. Bake at 350 degrees for 15 minutes or until done.

Turn out cake on a tea towel or cloth that has been sprinkled with 2 tablespoons of sugar. Roll up warm cake, from the long side, in the towel and let cool.

Wash and cap strawberries. Mix together 2 cups strawberries, cut very fine, with 1/4 cup of sugar. Unroll the cake and add sweetened strawberry mixture. Cut the remaining strawberries in halves to use for decoration. Reserve.

Roll up the cake, beginning from long side. Whip the cream until stiff. Frost cake roll with whipped cream. Garnish with reserved strawberries.

Yields: 10 to 12 servings

Margaret Young

◆ RAINBOW ◆
ICE CREAM CAKE

2   cups coconut cookie crumbs
4   ounces semi-sweet chocolate bits, chopped fine
1/3   cup chopped pecans
1/3   cup margarine or butter, melted
1   quart chocolate-mint ice cream, softened
1   quart vanilla ice cream, softened
1   quart strawberry ice cream, softened
       Whipped cream, optional
       Fresh strawberries for garnish, optional

Combine the cookie crumbs, chocolate, nuts and margarine, mixing well. Press one third of mixture into bottom of a spring-form pan. Freeze until firm.

Press the chocolate ice cream on top of the crumb mixture and freeze until firm. Press one third of cookie mixture on top of the chocolate ice cream. Freeze until firm. Press the vanilla ice cream on top of the crumb mixture and freeze until firm. Press one third of mixture on top of the vanilla ice cream. Freeze until firm. Press the strawberry ice cream on top of the cookie mixture and freeze until firm.

Serve topped with whipped cream and fresh strawberries for garnish.

Yields: 12 to 16 servings

Margaret Young

◆CHOCOLATE FROSTING◆

1	stick margarine or butter
2 1/2	1-ounce squares unsweetened chocolate
	Dash of salt
1	box confectioners' sugar
1/3	cup brewed black coffee

In a small sauce pan, melt the butter and chocolate. Add the salt and sugar. Add enough coffee to make the frosting the right spreading consistency.

Yields: frosting for 2-layer cake

Eleanor Helms

◆ CREAM CHEESE ◆ FROSTING

1/2	stick margarine or butter, softened
1	3 ounce package cream cheese, softened
1	box confectioners' sugar
1	teaspoon vanilla
	Milk

Cream the margarine and cream cheese. Add the sugar and vanilla. Add enough milk to make right spreading consistency.

Yields: frosting for 2-layer cake

Eleanor Helms

♦ BAKE SHOP ♦
FROSTING

1   *box confectioners' sugar*
1/2   *cup vegetable shortening*
1/4   *cup milk*
1/2   *teaspoon salt*
1   *teaspoon vanilla*

Cream together the sugar, shortening and milk. Add the salt and vanilla. With electric mixer, beat on high speed for 2 minutes.

Yields: frosting for 2-layer cake

Betty Young

♦ PIES ♦

Bob and Pat Rush
August, 1955

Parks and Eleanor Helms
March, 1959

Craig and Jackie Brown
December, 1959

Following her retirement, Granny devoted much of her time to her grandchildren–all ten of us. I was a frequent visitor at Granny's, always ready to help her make oatmeal cookies or go to the grocery store. She thought I was extremely bright and could read all of the packages in the store. (Instead, television commercials had taught me how to recognize many products).

One afternoon, Granny had me, her three year old granddaughter, in the buggy seat at the Colonial Grocery Store. At the check out counter, I noticed Tube Rose Snuff displayed near the cash register. That morning, I had seen a commercial, picturing a can of Tube Rose Snuff sitting beside a coffee cup; I had assumed that you put snuff in your coffee. Since I didn't think Granny had any Tube Rose, I helped myself to six cans–two of each color. You can imagine the scream I heard in the kitchen when Granny removed the cans of snuff from her grocery bag. I dashed to the bedroom and dove under the bed.

A few minutes later, Mom came looking for me and an explanation for my selections. She managed to listen to my tale without laughing, then left for the store to return my purchases. Granny was convinced that the store manager, a deacon at her baptist church, had seen her purchase the snuff. Mom explained to the manager her daughter's purchase and made him promise not to tell anyone about Mrs. Allen's snuff purchase. A few years ago, Mom gave me one of the Tube Rose cans which she had kept from my shopping spree. Today, I display my can of Tube Rose on a kitchen shelf, as a small reminder of my days with Granny.

◆ BROWN SUGAR PIE ◆

Easy to make and good!

1	box brown sugar
3/4	cup margarine or butter, melted
3/4	cup milk
3	eggs, slightly beaten
3	tablespoons all-purpose flour
1/2	teaspoon salt
1	teaspoon vanilla
1	9-inch unbaked pie shell

Preheat oven to 350 degrees. Combine the sugar, margarine, milk and eggs. Add the flour and salt to the sugar mixture. Add the vanilla. Pour into the unbaked pie crust.

Bake at 350 degrees for 45 minutes.

Yields: 6 to 8 servings

Eleanor Helms

◆LEMON MERINGUE PIE◆

Filling:

1 1/2	cups sugar
1/3	cup cornstarch
1 1/2	cups hot water
3	egg yolks, beaten
3	tablespoons margarine or butter
4	tablespoons lemon juice
1 1/3	tablespoons grated lemon rind
1	9-inch pie shell, baked

Meringue:

4	egg whites, at room temperature
1/2	teaspoon cream of tartar
1/4	cup plus 2 tablespoons sugar

To prepare the pie: Preheat oven to 400 degrees. Mix in a saucepan the sugar, cornstarch and hot water. Cook over moderate heat, stirring constantly, until mixture thickens and boils. Boil 1 minute. Beat a little of the hot mixture into the egg yolks. Then beat the egg yolk into the hot mixture in saucepan. Boil 1 minute longer, stirring constantly. Remove from heat. Continue stirring until smooth. Blend in the margarine, lemon juice, and grated lemon rind. Pour into the baked pie crust.

To prepare the meringue: Beat the egg whites and cream of tartar at high speed with an electric mixer for 1 minute. Gradually add the sugar, one tablespoon at a time, beating until stiff peaks form and sugar dissolves, approximately 2 to 4 minutes. Beat in the vanilla. Cover the pie with meringue, sealing to the edges. Bake at 400 degrees for 8 to 10 minutes, until a delicate brown. Serve as soon as cool.

Yields: 6 to 8 servings

Margaret Young

♦ CHERRY NUGGET PIE ♦

Crust:
1   *box vanilla wafers*
1   *stick margarine, melted*

Filling:
1   *can condensed milk*
1/4   *cup lemon juice*
1   *can sour pitted cherries, drained*
1   *cup chopped pecans*
1/2   *pint whipping cream*

To prepare the pie crust: Preheat oven to 350 degrees. Crush about 70 vanilla wafers. Add the margarine and mix well. Line the bottom and sides of two 9-inch pie pans with the vanilla wafer mix. Bake at 350 degrees about 10 minutes. Remove from the oven and cool.

To prepare pie filling: Mix the milk and lemon juice. Add the cherries and nuts. Whip the cream and fold into the cherry mixture. Pour the cherry mixture into the pie crust and refrigerate for 8 hours.

Yields: 6 to 8 servings

Eleanor Helms

◆ REQUEST CHERRY PIE ◆

1	cup sugar
3	tablespoons cornstarch
1/4	teaspoon salt
1	cup juice from cherries
1/4	teaspoon red food coloring
1/8	teaspoon almond extract, optional
2	16-ounce cans water packed, tart, pitted cherries, drained
2	tablespoons margarine or butter, melted
1	9-inch, 2-crust pie shell

Preheat oven to 425 degrees. Mix the sugar, cornstarch and salt in a saucepan. Add the juice, coloring and almond extract. Stir until smooth. Cook, stirring constantly, until thickened and clear.

Remove the sauce from heat. Stir in the cherries and margarine. Pour into an unbaked pie crust. Cover with a lattice top crust.

Bake at 425 degrees for 40 minutes.

Yields: 6 to 8 servings

Margaret Young

♦ CHERRY PIE ♦

1	*16-ounce can red, tart, pitted cherries*
2/3	*cup sugar*
2	*tablespoons cornstarch*
1/4	*teaspoon salt*
1/2	*teaspoon cinnamon, optional*
2	*tablespoons margarine or butter*
1	*8-inch 2-crust pie shell*

Preheat oven to 400 degrees. In a saucepan, heat the drained liquid from the cherries to boiling Sift the sugar, cornstarch, salt and cinnamon into the boiling liquid. Cook until thick and clear, stirring constantly. Add the margarine and cherries and pour into an uncooked pie crust. Cover top with crust. Bake at 400 degrees about 30 minutes or until crust browns.

Yields: 6 to 8 servings

Margaret Young

♦ STRAWBERRY ♦
GLAZE PIE

1	9-inch pie shell
1	quart fresh strawberries, washed, capped and sliced
1	cup sugar
3	tablespoons cornstarch
1	cup water
	Red food coloring
	Whipping cream

Bake the pie shell according to directions and let cool.

Mix the sugar and cornstarch in a 2-quart saucepan. Stir in the water gradually until smooth. Add 1 cup strawberries. Cook over medium heat, stirring until thick and clear. Stir in a few drops red food color. Cool. Stir in the remaining strawberries, reserving 1/4 cup for garnish. Pour strawberry mixture into the pie shell. Chill until firm, about 3 hours.

Serve topped with whipping cream and garnished with the remaining berries.

Yields: 6 to 8 servings

Margaret Young

♦ STRAWBERRY PIE ♦

3   cups sliced strawberries
3/4   cup sugar
1   tablespoon cornstarch
1/2   small package dry strawberry Jello
1/2   stick margarine
1   2-crust pie crust

Preheat oven to 400 degrees. Put the strawberries in an un-cooked pie crust. Mix the sugar, cornstarch, and dry Jello to-gether; pour on top of the strawberries. Add 1/4 stick of margarine cut in small pieces on top of mixture. Cover the top of pie with the second pie crust and dot the crust with 1/4 stick margarine.

Bake at 400 degrees for approximately 25 minutes. Reduce the temperature to 350 degrees and cook until crust is brown.

Yields: 6 to 8 servings

Ida Helms

◆ Fresh Peach Pie ◆

1   cup sugar
2   tablespoons all-purpose flour
1/4   teaspoon salt
8   peaches, peeled and sliced
1/3   cup margarine or butter
1   2-crust pie shell

Preheat oven to 475 degrees. Blend the sugar, flour and salt. Mix with peaches. Place the peach mixture into an unbaked pie shell. Add the top crust. Dot generously with margarine.

Bake at 475 degrees for 15 minutes. Reduce the temperature to 400 degrees and bake for 30 to 35 minutes. If the crust gets too brown, cover pie with foil.

Yields: 6 to 8 servings

Margaret Young

◆ Peach Glaze Pie ◆

8	fresh peaches, peeled and sliced
1	9-inch pie crust, baked
3/4	cup sugar (or more if desired)
6	teaspoons cornstarch
1	cup water
1	3-ounce box peach gelatin
	Whipped cream

Place the peaches into the baked pie shell.

In a saucepan, mix together the sugar, cornstarch and water. Cook until thick and clear and add the peach gelatin. Pour the mixture over peaches. Refrigerate the pie until cold. Serve the pie with whipped topping or whipped cream.

Yields: 6 to 8 servings

Margaret Young

◆ EASY PEACH COBBLER ◆

Great when peaches are in season.

3	cups sliced peaches
1 1/2	cups sugar
1/2	stick margarine
3/4	cup all-purpose flour
1	teaspoon baking powder
	Dash salt
3/4	cup milk

Preheat oven to 350 degrees. Mix the peaches with 1 cup sugar and set aside.

Put the margarine in an 8-inch pan and place in the oven to melt. Mix 1/2 cup sugar, flour and baking powder, salt and milk. Spoon the flour batter over melted margarine. Do not stir. Place sugared peaches on top of batter. Do not stir.

Bake at 350 degrees for 1 hour. The crust will rise to top during baking.

Yields: 8 to 10 servings

Pat Rush

◆ PEACH ◆
CHIFFON DESSERT

1/3	cup cornstarch
1/2	cup sugar
1/4	teaspoon salt
2	cups milk
2	egg yolks, slightly beaten
2 1/2	cups sliced fresh peaches
1/2	cup water
1	teaspoon lemon juice
1/2	teaspoon vanilla
2	egg whites
2	tablespoons sugar
1/2	cup whipped cream, optional

In a medium saucepan stir together cornstarch, 1/2 cup sugar and salt. Gradually stir in the milk until smooth. Stir in the egg yolks. Bring to a boil over medium low heat, stirring constantly and boil for 1 minute. Remove from heat.

In a blender, place 2 cups of peaches, water, lemon juice and vanilla. Blend on high speed 60 seconds or until mixture is pureed. Pour peach mixture into a medium bowl. Stir in the cornstarch mixture.

In a small bowl, beat egg whites until foamy. Gradually add 2 tablespoons sugar. Beat until stiff peaks form when beater is raised. Fold into the peach mixture. Stir in the remaining 1/2 cup of sliced peaches. Spoon into individual dessert dishes. Chill. If desired, garnish with whipped cream.

Yields: 12 servings

Margaret Young

♦ BLACKBERRY ♦
CREAM PIE

1	cup sugar
1	cup sour cream
3	tablespoons all-purpose flour
1/4	teaspoon salt
1	16 ounce package frozen blackberries, thawed or 4 cups fresh blackberries
1	9-inch pie shell, unbaked
1/4 to 1/2	cup fine dry bread crumbs
2	tablespoons sugar
1	tablespoon margarine or butter, melted

Preheat oven to 375 degrees. Combine the sugar, sour cream, flour and salt. Place blackberries in the pie shell. Spread the sour cream mixture over top. In a small bowl, combine the bread crumbs, 2 tablespoons sugar, and margarine. Sprinkle the bread crumb mixture over the sour cream mixture.

Bake at 375 degrees for 40 to 45 minutes or until done.

Yields: 6 to 8 servings

Ida Helms

♦ APPLE CRUMB PIE ♦

Pie filling:
5 to 6   *cups sliced apples (about 6 apples)*
1 1/2   *tablespoons water (if apples are dry)*
1 1/2   *teaspoons cinnamon*

Crumb Topping:
1   *stick margarine*
1   *cup sugar*
1   *cup all-purpose flour*

Preheat oven to 350 degrees. Put the apples in a deep dish. If the apples are dry, sprinkle water over the apples and gently toss. Sprinkle the cinnamon over the apples.

Cut the margarine, sugar and flour with a pastry blender or fork till crumbly. Pour topping over the apples.

Bake at 350 degrees for 45 minutes.

Yields: 6 to 8 servings

Margaret Young

◆ TRISHA'S HOMEMADE ◆ APPLE PIE

Pie Crust:
2	cups all-purpose flour
1	teaspoon salt
3/4	cup vegetable shortening
4 to 5	tablespoons ice water

Filling:
5 to 6	Granny Smith Apples, peeled and sliced
5	tablespoons all-purpose flour
1 1/4	cups sugar
1	teaspoon cinnamon
	Sprinkle of nutmeg (to taste)
1	tablespoon margarine or butter
1	teaspoon lemon juice

To prepare pie crust: With pastry blender or fork, cut the flour, salt, shortening and ice water. Gather the dough together and press firmly into a ball. Roll out into a circle 1-inch larger than pan all around. Fit pastry loosely into the pan. Trim off edges with scissors, leaving 1/2 inch overhanging edge of pan. Fold extra pastry back and under to build a high fluted edge. Reserve dough for lattice for the top of the pie.

To prepare pie filling: Preheat oven to 400 degrees. Pour the apples into the unbaked pie crust. Mix flour, sugar, cinnamon and nutmeg and sprinkle over apples. Dot with margarine and sprinkle with lemon juice for flavor. Top with pie crust and sprinkle crust with sugar. Vent the pie crust. Bake 15 minutes at 400 degrees, reduce heat to 350 degrees and bake for 45 minutes.

Yields: 8 servings

Patricia Weeks

♦ CREAMY SWEET ♦ POTATO PIE

A holiday tradition.

2	cups mashed sweet potatoes
1	14-ounce can sweetened condensed milk
2	eggs
1	teaspoon cinnamon
1/2	teaspoon salt
1/2	teaspoon ginger
1/2	teaspoon nutmeg
1	9-inch unbaked pie shell
	Whipped cream for garnish

Preheat oven to 425 degrees. Combine the potatoes, milk, eggs, cinnamon, salt, ginger, and nutmeg. Mix well and pour into the pie shell. Bake at 425 degrees for 15 minutes. Reduce the temperature to 350 degrees and bake for 35 to 50 minutes, or until a knife comes out clean. Garnish with whipped cream before cutting.

Yields: 6 to 8 servings

Margaret Young

◆ PECAN PIE ◆

Easy!

3   eggs, beaten
2/3   cup light brown sugar
1   teaspoon all-purpose flour
1/3   teaspoon salt
1/3   cup margarine or butter
1   cup white corn syrup
1   teaspoon vanilla
1   cup pecans, chopped
1   9-inch pie shell

Preheat oven to 350 degrees. Combine the eggs, sugar, flour, and salt. Mix well. Add the margarine, syrup and vanilla. Add the pecans. Pour into an unbaked pie crust.

Bake at 350 degrees for 1 hour.

Yields: 6 to 8 servings

Eleanor Helms

◆ PINEAPPLE ◆
COCONUT PIE

1 2/3   cups sugar
3   heaping tablespoons all-purpose flour
1   stick margarine, melted
4   eggs
1   teaspoon vanilla
1   small can crushed pineapple with heavy syrup
1   7-ounce bag coconut
1   9-inch pie crust, unbaked

Preheat the oven to 350 degrees. Combine the sugar and flour. Add the margarine and mix well. Add the eggs, one at a time, stirring after each addition. Add the vanilla, pineapple and coconut and mix well.

Pour the coconut mixture into the pie crust and bake at 350 degrees for 1 hour or until golden brown and firm.

Yields: 6 to 8 servings

Eleanor Helms

◆ COCONUT PIE ◆

1	6-ounce package frozen coconut
1	9-inch pie crust, unbaked
1 1/4	cups sugar
3	eggs
1	teaspoon vanilla
1/3 to 1/2	stick margarine or butter, melted
2	small cans evaporated milk

Preheat oven to 400 degrees. Put coconut in bottom of a pie crust.

Mix the sugar, eggs, vanilla, margarine and milk and pour over coconut. Cook at 400 degrees for 30 to 40 minutes until firm.

Yields: 6 to 8 servings

Ida Helms

♦ PINEAPPLE DREAM PIE ♦

1 1/3	cups flaked coconut
2	tablespoons margarine or butter, melted
1	3 ounce package lemon-flavored gelatin
1	3 1/4 ounce package vanilla tapioca pudding mix
1 1/4	cups milk
1/3	cup frozen unsweetened pineapple juice concentrate, thawed
1	2 or 2 1/8-ounce package dessert topping mix
1	8 3/4-ounce can crushed pineapple, well drained

Preheat oven to 325 degrees. Combine coconut and margarine and press on bottom and sides of 9-inch pie crust. Bake at 325 degrees for 15 minutes, until coconut is golden. Cool.

In a medium saucepan, combine the gelatin and pudding mix. Stir in the milk. Cook and stir until mixture boils. Remove from heat. Stir in pineapple juice and chill until partially set. Prepare the dessert topping mix according to package directions. Fold into pudding mixture. Add pineapple. Pour into pie crust. Refrigerate for 5 to 6 hours.

Yields: 6 to 8 servings

Margaret Young

♦ BANANA CREAM PIE ♦

1/2	cup sugar
6	tablespoons all-purpose flour
1/4	teaspoon salt
2 1/2	cups milk
1	egg
1	tablespoon margarine or butter
1/2	teaspoon lemon extract
2	ripe bananas
1	9-inch pie shell, baked
1/2	cup shredded coconut
1/2	cup heavy cream, whipped

Preheat oven to 350 degrees. Mix the sugar, flour and salt in top of double boiler. Gradually stir in the milk and cook over boiling water until thickened, stirring constantly. Cover, and cook for 10 minutes longer, stirring occasionally.

Beat the egg and add a small amount of the hot milk mixture. Add the egg to the double boiler and cook for two minutes over hot, not boiling water, stirring constantly. Remove from heat, and add the margarine and lemon extract. Let cool.

Slice two bananas into a baked pie shell. Pour the cooked mixture over bananas at once. Chill for at least one hour. Place coconut in a shallow pan and toast by baking at 350 degrees for 10 minutes or until lightly browned, stirring occasionally. Let cool. Top pie with whipped cream and toasted coconut.

Yields: 6 to 8 servings

Margaret Young

♦ BANANA SPLIT PIE ♦

2	graham cracker crumb crusts
1	stick margarine
1	8-ounce package cream cheese
3/4	box of confectioners' sugar
3	bananas, sliced
1	large can crushed pineapple, drained slightly
1	cup chopped pecans
1/2	cup whipped cream
	Coconut for garnish

Combine the margarine, cream cheese and sugar. Beat until creamed. Spread on the bottom of 2 graham cracker crust pie pans.

In the following order, layer the bananas, pineapple, pecans, and whipped cream. Sprinkle coconut on top as garnish.

Refrigerate for 6 to 8 hours.

Yields: 12 servings

Margaret Young

◆ BANANA COCONUT ◆ CHIFFON PIE

1	*envelope unflavored gelatin*
1/4	*cup cold water*
3	*eggs, separated*
1	*cup mashed, ripe bananas (3 medium)*
1/3	*cup sugar*
1/4	*teaspoon salt*
1/2	*cup heavy cream*
1/3	*cup finely grated fresh or frozen coconut*
1	*9-inch pie crust, baked*

Soften the gelatin in cold water. Slightly beat the egg yolks in top of double boiler. Stir in the bananas, sugar and salt. Cook over boiling water, stirring constantly, until slightly thickened. Remove from heat. Add the softened gelatin and stir until dissolved. Chill until the mixture is slightly thickened.

Beat the egg whites until stiff but not dry. Beat the cream until stiff. Fold the egg whites, cream and coconut into banana mixture.

Pour into the pie crust and chill until firm. Garnish with additional whipped cream and sliced bananas if desired.

Yields: 6 to 8 servings

Margaret Young

◆ MOM'S ◆
CHOCOLATE PIE

Pie Filling:

1	*cup sugar*
3/4	*cup all-purpose flour*
3	*tablespoons cocoa*
1	*small can condensed milk*
3	*eggs, separated*
2	*cups milk*
2	*9-inch pie shells, baked*

Meringue

3 to 4	*egg whites*
1/4 to 1/2	*cup sugar*

In a sauce pan, combine the sugar, flour and cocoa. Add the condensed milk, egg yolks, and milk. Cook over medium high heat until mixture becomes slightly thickened. Do not overcook! Pour the mixture into the baked pie shells. Set aside.

Beat the egg whites until fluffy. Add 1/4 to 1/2 cup sugar and beat. Top the pies with the meringue. Bake at 400 degrees until meringue is browned.

Yields: 12 servings

Janet Allen

◆ IMPOSSIBLE ◆
CHOCOLATE CREAM PIE

2	eggs
1	cup milk
1/4	cup margarine or butter, softened
1	teaspoon vanilla
2	1-ounce squares melted unsweetened chocolate, cooled
1	cup sugar
1/2	cup Bisquick baking mix
1	cup chilled whipped cream
2	tablespoons sugar

Preheat the oven to 350 degrees. Grease a 9-inch pie pan.

Place the eggs, milk, margarine, vanilla, chocolate, sugar and baking mix into a blender container. Cover and blend on high for 1 minute. Pour the mixture into the pie pan. Bake at 350 degrees for 30 minutes, until no indentation remains when touched lightly in center. Cool completely.

Whip the chilled whipping cream and 2 tablespoons sugar until stiff. Top the pie with whipped cream.

Yields: 6 to 8 servings

Margaret Young

♦ CHOCOLATE ♦
CREAM PIE

1 1/2	cups sugar
1/2	teaspoon salt
2 1/2	tablespoons cornstarch
1	tablespoon all-purpose flour
3	cups milk
3	1-ounce squares unsweetened chocolate
3	egg yolks, slightly beaten
1	tablespoon margarine or butter
1 1/2	teaspoons vanilla
1	9-inch pie crust, baked and cooled
1/2	cup whipping cream
1	tablespoon confectioners' sugar
1/4	teaspoon vanilla
	Shaved nuts, toasted coconut or fresh berries

In saucepan, combine the sugar, salt, cornstarch and flour. Gradually stir in the milk, while heating. Add the chocolate and stir until chocolate melts. Cook over moderate heat, stirring constantly, until mixture thickens and boils. Boil 1 minute.

Remove from heat. Stir a little of the mixture into the egg yolks. Then blend egg yolks into hot mixture in saucepan. Boil 1 minute more, stirring constantly. Remove from heat. Blend in the margarine and vanilla. Cool, stirring occasionally. Pour into the pie shell. Chill thoroughly for 2 hours.

Whip the whipping cream stiff, beat in the sugar and vanilla. Garnish with shaved nuts, toasted coconut, or fresh berries. Remove pie from refrigerator 20 minutes before serving.

Yields: 8 servings

Margaret Young

♦ FUDGE PIE ♦

2	squares unsweetened chocolate, melted
1	stick margarine or butter
1 1/4	cups sugar
1/4	cup evaporated milk
2	eggs
1	teaspoon vanilla
1	9-inch pie shell, unbaked

Preheat oven to 325 degrees. Combine the chocolate, margarine, sugar, milk, eggs and vanilla over low heat. Pour into a 9-inch unbaked pie shell. Bake at 325 degrees for 40 minutes.

Yields: 6 to 8 servings

Jackie Brown

♦ BROWNIE PIE ♦

3	egg whites
3/4	cup sugar
	Dash salt
3/4	cup fine chocolate cookie crumbs (14 cookies)
1/2	cup chopped nuts
1/2	teaspoon vanilla
1	cup whipping cream
1	1-ounce unsweetened chocolate square, optional

Preheat oven to 325 degrees. Lightly grease a 9-inch pie pan. Beat the egg whites until soft peaks form. Gradually add the sugar, beating until stiff peaks form. Fold in the salt, crumbs, nuts and vanilla. Spread the mixture evenly in the pie pan.

Bake at 325 degrees about 30 minutes. Cool thoroughly. Spread with sweetened whipped cream. Chill well for 3 to 4 hours. Garnish with chocolate curls shaved from unsweetened chocolate square.

Yields: 6 to 8 servings

Eleanor Helms

♦ TRISHA'S OREO PIE ♦

1	16-ounce package of Oreo cookies, crushed
1	stick margarine or butter, melted
1	8-ounce package cream cheese, softened
1	12-ounce Cool Whip, softened
1	large package of instant chocolate pudding
2 1/2	cups milk

Mix the cookie crumbs with the melted margarine. Reserve 1/2 cup of cookie mixture for topping. Press the remaining cookie mixture into the bottom of a 13x9-inch pan.

Cream together 6 ounces Cool Whip and cream cheese, spread over cookies. Mix the milk with the pudding and spread over the creamed mixture. Take the remaining Cool Whip and spread over pudding. Sprinkle the reserved cookie mixture on top.

Yields: 12 servings

Patricia Weeks

◆ IMPOSSIBLE ◆
CHEESECAKE PIE

Cheesecake:
3/4	cup milk
2	teaspoons vanilla
2	eggs
1	cup sugar
1/2	cup Bisquick baking mix
2	8-ounce packages cream cheese, cut into 1/2-inch cubes, softened

Topping:
1	cup sour cream
2	tablespoons sugar
2	teaspoons vanilla

To prepare the pie: Preheat oven to 350 degrees. Grease a 9-inch pie pan.

Place milk, vanilla, eggs, sugar and baking mix in blender container. Cover and blend on high 15 seconds. Add the cream cheese. Cover and blend on high 2 minutes. Pour into the pie pan. Bake at 350 degrees for 40 to 45 minutes, until center is firm. Let cool.

To prepare the topping: Mix the sour cream, sugar and vanilla. Spread the topping carefully over top of cheesecake. Garnish with fruit if desired.

Yields: 6 to 8 servings

Margaret Young

◆ LIGHT 'N FRUITY PIE ◆

1   3-ounce package Jello brand gelatin, any fruit flavor
2/3   cup boiling water
2   cups ice cubes
3 1/2   cups Cool Whip, thawed
1   9-inch graham cracker crumb crust

Dissolve the gelatin completely in boiling water, stirring about 3 minutes. Add the ice cubes and stir constantly until gelatin is thickened, about 2 to 3 minutes. Remove any unmelted ice. Using wire whisk, blend in the whipped topping. Whip until smooth. Chill, if necessary, until mixture will mound. Spoon into pie crust. Chill for 2 hours.

Garnish with lime slice, if desired.

Yields: 6 to 8 servings

Margaret Young

◆ CREPES ◆

*Wonderful, light crepes which can be
filled with fresh fruit and topped
with whipped cream or ice cream.*

1	cup cold water
1	cup cold milk
4	eggs
1/2	teaspoon salt
2	cups all-purpose flour, sifted
4	tablespoons melted margarine or butter

Put the water, milk, eggs, and salt into a blender container. Add the flour, then the margarine. Cover and blend at top speed for 1 minute. If the flour adheres to sides of jar, dislodge with a rubber scraper and blend for 2 to 3 seconds more. Cover and refrigerate for at least 2 hours.

The batter should be a very light cream consistency, just thick enough to coat a wooden spoon. If, after making the first crepe, it seems to heavy, beat in a bit of water, a spoonful at a time. A cooked crepe should be about 1/16 inch thick.

Yields: 12 crepes

Margaret Young

◆ ONE CRUST ◆ PIE SHELL

1	cup all-purpose flour, sifted
1/2	teaspoon salt
1/3	cup vegetable shortening
2	tablespoons water

Preheat oven to 450 degrees. Mix together the flour and salt. Cut the flour into the shortening with a pastry blender. Sprinkle with water.

Gather the dough together and press firmly into a ball. Roll out into a circle 1" larger than pan all around. Fit the pastry loosely into pan. Avoid stretching to prevent shrinking.

Trim off ragged edges with scissors, leaving 1/2" overhanging edge of pan. Fold extra pastry back and under, and build up a high fluted edge.

Yields: 1 one-crust pie shell

Margaret Young

◆ NEVER FAIL ◆
PIE CRUST

3   *cups all-purpose flour*
1 1/4   *cups vegetable shortening*
1   *tablespoon sugar*
1 to 2   *teaspoons salt*
1   *egg*
1   *tablespoon vinegar*
1/2   *cup water*

Mix the flour, shortening, sugar and salt with a pastry blender or a fork. In a bowl, beat the egg, add the water and vinegar and mix well. Combine the two mixtures, a little at a time until all the dry ingredients are moist. Mold together with your hands.

Chill before rolling. Dough may be kept in the refrigerator up to a week. The dough may be frozen and later used after returning the dough to room temperature.

Bake the unfilled crust in a 450 degree oven until lightly browned.

Yields: two 9-inch 2-crust pie shells and one 9-inch shell

Margaret Young

◆ FLAKY PIE CRUST ◆

2   cups all-purpose flour, sifted
1   teaspoon salt
3/4   cup vegetable shortening
4 to 5 tablespoons cold water

Preheat oven to 450 degrees. Mix flour and salt. Cut in shortening until the shortening is finely dispersed through the flour. Add the water, a tablespoon at a time. Mix well and add more water to driest portion each time.

When dough is moist enough to hold together (it should not be sticky), gather it up, form into a ball and roll out for pastry. Dough may be kept in refrigerator until ready to use.

Bake the unfilled crust in a 450 degree oven until lightly browned. Cool and fill.

Yields: one 8 or 9-inch 2-crust pie shell

Margaret Young

♦ EGG YOLK PIE CRUST ♦

5	cups all-purpose flour, sifted
3	teaspoons sugar
1/2	teaspoon salt
1/2	teaspoon baking powder
1 1/2	cups shortening
2	egg yolks
	Cold water

Preheat oven to 450 degrees. Combine the flour, sugar, salt, and baking powder. Cut in the shortening.

Beat the egg yolks slightly in measuring cup with fork and blend in enough cold water to make a scant cupful. Add to dry mixture and mix. Roll out like any pastry.

Bake the unfilled pastry in a 450 degree oven until slightly browned.

Yields: three 2-crust 9-inch pies

Margaret Young

◆ COOKIES ◆
AND DESSERTS

Bennett Alston

Here's a look to the future-- one of Granny's great grandchildren. Bennett was named after his great grandfather, Paul Bennett Allen.

Granny lived a rich life, full of family and friends who loved her. As she declined with Alzheimer's, we moved Granny to a nursing home for 24 hour care. Each day, one of her daughters went to feed her lunch and visit with her for few hours.

One afternoon, Eleanor took Granny outside to enjoy a beautiful, sunny day. Granny looked across the yard at a stranger and asked, "Is that Karen there?" Eleanor called me from her car phone, overjoyed that Granny had spoken a full sentence. I said a silent prayer, grateful that I was alive and well in her heart.

Ten grandchildren led to five great-grandchildren. Granny loved the great grandchildren's visits to the nursing home. Bennett, my grandfather's namesake and my godson, visited often to eat ice cream with Granny. Those were some of Granny's happiest days and our fondest memories of the Wesley Nursing Center.

◆ GREAT ◆
GRANDMOTHER'S
SUGAR COOKIES

2 1/4	cups all-purpose flour, sifted
1/4	teaspoon salt
2	teaspoons baking powder
1/2	stick margarine
1/4	cup shortening
1	cup sugar
2	eggs, beaten
1/2	teaspoon vanilla
1	tablespoon milk
1/2	cup ground walnuts, optional
	Sugar

Preheat the oven to 375 degrees. Sift together the flour, salt and baking powder.

Cream the shortening, margarine and sugar together. Add the eggs, vanilla and sifted ingredients. Add the milk and mix well. Add the nuts. Roll out the dough and cut cookies. Sprinkle with sugar.

Bake on greased cookie sheet at 375 degrees for 12 minutes.

Yields: 60 cookies

Cynthia Biggers
Ruth Biggers

◆ RANGER COOKIES ◆

1	stick margarine
1/2	cup shortening
1	cup sugar
1 1/2	teaspoons vanilla
2	eggs, slightly beaten
1	cup brown sugar
2	cups all-purpose flour
1	teaspoon baking soda
1/2	teaspoon salt
1/2	teaspoon baking powder
2	cups rolled oats
	Nuts, coconut or raisins

Preheat oven to 350 degrees. Combine the margarine and shortening. Add the sugar, vanilla, eggs, and brown sugar and mix well. Sift the flour, baking soda, salt and baking powder together. Slowly add the dry ingredients to the creamed mixture. Add the rolled oats and stir well. Add your choice of nuts, coconut or raisins.

Bake at 350 degrees for 10 to 12 minutes.

Yields: 36 cookies

Janet Allen

◆ PEANUT BUTTER ◆ KISS COOKIES

1	18-ounce jar smooth peanut butter
1 1/2	cups sugar
2	eggs, slightly beaten
1	9-ounce package chocolate kisses

Preheat oven to 350 degrees. Mix the peanut butter, sugar and eggs with a wooden spoon.

Flour hands and roll mixture into balls. On greased cookie sheet, place balls 1 1/2-inches apart. Bake at 350 degrees for 12 to 14 minutes.

While still hot, place chocolate kiss in the middle of each cookie. Remove cookies from cookie sheet and let cookies cool completely. Store in an air tight container.

Yields: 48 cookies

Betty Young

♦ CHOCOLATE CHIP ♦ COOKIES

Pat's chocolate chip cookies are a family treasure, which we all love-young and old alike. She refrigerates her dough and bakes them just before serving, so they're always fresh.

2/3	cup vegetable shortening
2/3	cup margarine
1	cup sugar
1	cup brown sugar
2	eggs
2	teaspoons vanilla
3 1/2	cups all-purpose flour
1	teaspoon baking soda
3/4	teaspoon salt
1	cup nuts, optional
1	12-ounce package semi-sweet chocolate chips

Preheat the oven to 375 degrees. Mix thoroughly the shortening, margarine, sugar, brown sugar, eggs and vanilla. Sift together the flour, baking soda and salt. Add the dry ingredients to the creamed mixture. Stir in the nuts and chocolate chips.

Drop on an ungreased cookie sheet by rounded teaspoonfuls about 2-inches apart. Bake at 375 degrees for 8 to 10 minutes. Bake until lightly browned. Cookies should still be soft. Cool slightly before removing from cookie sheet.

Yields: 48 cookies

Pat Rush

◆ OATMEAL COOKIES ◆

*I "helped" Granny makes these cookies once,
by adding a tablespoon of salt--rather than a
teaspoon. (They were pretty bad). When you get the
measurements right, these cookies will melt in your mouth.*

1/2	cup vegetable shortening
1 1/4	cups sugar
1/2	cup molasses
2	eggs
1 3/4	cup all-purpose flour
1	teaspoon salt
1	teaspoon baking soda
1	teaspoon cinnamon
2	cups oatmeal
1 1/2	cups raisins

Preheat oven to 375 degrees. Beat the shortening, sugar, molasses and eggs. Sift together the flour, salt, baking soda, and cinnamon. Add the dry ingredients to the creamed mixture. Stir in oatmeal and raisins.

Drop on lightly greased cookie sheet by teaspoonfuls. Bake at 375 degrees for 8 to 10 minutes.

Yields: 48 cookies

Gladys Allen
Pat Rush

◆ BUTTERMILK ◆
OATMEAL COOKIES

1	cup vegetable shortening
1 1/2	cups brown sugar
2	eggs
1/2	cup buttermilk*
1 1/2	cups all-purpose flour, sifted
1	teaspoon baking soda*
1	teaspoon baking powder*
1	teaspoon salt
1	teaspoon cinnamon
1	teaspoon nutmeg
3	cups quick-cooking rolled oats
1/2 to 1	cup seedless raisins
	Walnut halves, optional

Preheat oven to 400 degrees. Cream together the shortening, brown sugar, and eggs until light and fluffy. Stir in the buttermilk.

Sift together the flour, baking soda, baking powder, salt, and spices; stir into creamed mixture. Stir in the rolled oats and the raisins. Drop from tablespoon 2-inches apart on greased cookie sheet. Top each with walnut half, if desired.

Bake at 400 degrees about 10 minutes or till lightly browned.

* *Variation:* In lieu of buttermilk, substitute with 1/2 cup milk; cut baking soda to 1/4 teaspoon and increase the baking powder to 2 teaspoons.

Yields: 48 cookies

Margaret Young

♦ MOLASSES COOKIES ♦

3/4	cup shortening
1	cup sugar
1/4	cup dark or light molasses
1	egg
2	cups all-purpose flour
2	teaspoons soda
1/2	teaspoon salt
1/2	teaspoon clove
1/2	teaspoon ginger
1	teaspoon cinnamon
	Granulated sugar

Preheat oven to 375 degrees. Melt the shortening and let it cool to room temperature. Add the sugar, molasses and egg and beat well.

Sift the flour with the baking soda, salt and spices, and add dry ingredients to the shortening mixture. Chill the dough. Take out a teaspoon of the dough, roll it into a ball. Roll the ball in granulated sugar.

Place the cookie balls on a greased baking sheet and bake at 375 degrees for 8 to 15 minutes, until they are light brown. Loosen from the pan while still quite warm, and cool in a single layer on a rack.

Yields: 48 cookies

Margaret Young

◆ NEIMAN-MARCUS ◆ $250 COOKIE RECIPE

4   sticks butter
2   cups granulated sugar
2   cups brown sugar
4   eggs
2   teaspoons vanilla
5   cups oatmeal
4   cups all-purpose flour
1   teaspoon salt
2   teaspoons baking powder
2   teaspoons baking soda
2   12 ounce bags chocolate chips
1   8-ounce bar Hershey unsweetened chocolate, coarsely grated
3   cups chopped nuts

Preheat oven to 375 degrees. Cream the butter and both sugars. Add the eggs and vanilla. With blender, process the oatmeal to a fine powder. Mix together the creamed mixture with oatmeal, flour, salt, baking powder and baking soda. Add the chocolate chips, unsweetened chocolate and nuts. Roll into balls and place two inches apart on a cookie sheet. Bake at 375 degrees for 6 minutes.

Note: Recipe will halve perfectly.

Yields: 112 cookies

Jackie Brown

♦ NO-BAKE ♦
ICE BOX COOKIES

Cookies:

1	box graham crackers, crushed
1	cup margarine or butter
1	cup sugar
1	egg
1/2	cup milk
1	cup nuts
1	cup coconut
1	cup graham cracker crumbs

Icing:

6	tablespoons margarine or butter
2	cups confectioners' sugar
1	tablespoon milk
1	teaspoon vanilla

To prepare the cookies: Line a 9x13-inch pan with graham crackers. Melt the butter. Beat the sugar, egg, and milk together, and add to melted butter and bring mixture to a boil. Remove from heat and add the nuts, coconut, and cracker crumbs. Pour in pan over layer of graham crackers. Top with another layer of crackers.

To prepare the icing: Combine the margarine, sugar, milk and vanilla. Ice the cookies and refrigerate for 2 to 24 hours.

Yields: 24 bars

Martha Helms

◆ CHERRY CHEWBILEES ◆

Crust:
1   cup walnut pieces, divided
1 1/4 cups all-purpose flour
1/2   cup firmly packed brown sugar
1/2   cup Butter Flavored Crisco
1/2   cup flake coconut

Filling:
2   8-ounce packages cream cheese, softened
2/3   cup granulated sugar
2   eggs
2   teaspoons vanilla
1   21-ounce can cherry pie filling

Preheat oven to 350 degrees. Grease a 13x9-inch pan with the Crisco and set aside.

To prepare the crust: Chop 1/2 cup nuts coarsely for topping and set aside. Chop remaining 1/2 cup finely. For crust, combine the flour and brown sugar. Cut in the Crisco until fine crumbs form. Add 1/2 cup finely chopped nuts and coconut and mix well. Remove 1/2 cup of mixture and set aside. Press remaining crumbs in bottom of pan. Bake at 350 degrees for 12 to 15 minutes, until edges are lightly browned.

To prepare the filling: Beat the cream cheese, sugar, eggs and vanilla and pour into the baked crust. Bake at 350 degrees for 15 minutes. Spread the cherry pie filling over the cheese layer. Combine reserved coarsely chopped nuts and reserved crumbs and sprinkle evenly over the cherries. Bake at 350 degrees for an additional 15 minutes. Let cool and refrigerate for several hours. Cut into bars.

Yields: 36 bars

Margaret Young

◆ Ooey-Gooey ◆
Cheese Cake

4   *eggs*
1   *yellow cake mix*
1   *stick margarine, melted*
1   *8-ounce package cream cheese, at room temperature*
1   *box confectioners' sugar*

Preheat oven to 350 degrees. To prepare the first layer, beat two eggs until foamy. Add the cake mix and margarine. Mix well. Pour the cake mixture into a greased and floured 13x9-inch pan.

For the second layer, beat two eggs until foamy. Add the cream cheese and sugar, mixing well. Pour the cream cheese mixture on top of the first layer.

Bake at 350 degrees for 40 minutes. The cake will fall after it comes out of the oven, which is normal. Cool for 2 hours. Cut into squares.

Variation: Use a lemon cake mix for lemon flavor.

Yields: 8 to 10 servings

Betty Young

♦ Blackberry ♦ Dumplings

1   *quart fresh or frozen blackberries*
1   *cup plus 1 tablespoon sugar, divided*
3/4   *teaspoon salt, divided*
1/2   *teaspoon lemon extract*
1 1/2 *cups all-purpose flour*
2   *teaspoons baking powder*
1/4   *teaspoon ground nutmeg*
2/3   *cup milk*
      Cream or whipped cream, optional

Preheat oven to 400 degrees. In a Dutch oven, combine the blackberries, 1 cup sugar, 1/4 teaspoon salt, and lemon extract. Bring to a boil. Reduce heat and simmer for 5 minutes.

In a mixing bowl, combine the flour, baking powder, nutmeg, 1 tablespoon sugar, and remaining salt. Add the milk. Stir just until mixed. Dough will be very thick. Drop by tablespoonfuls into six mounds onto hot blackberry mixture. Bake at 400 degrees for 35 to 45 minutes.

Variation: Substitute a 9-inch pie crust for the dumpling mixture.

Yields: 6 servings

Pat Rush

♦ BENNETT'S ♦
BANANA PUDDING

1/2	cup sugar
1/3	cup all-purpose flour
1/2	cup evaporated milk
1/2	cup water
3	egg yolks
1	teaspoon vanilla
2	tablespoon margarine
	Vanilla wafers
	Bananas, sliced
3	egg whites
1/4	cup sugar
1/4	teaspoon cream of tartar

Combine the sugar and flour in a medium saucepan. Add the milk and water, slowly, using a whisk to dissolve the flour before putting on the stove top. Heat, stirring continuously to avoid scorching. Add the egg yolks and margarine. Stir until thickened.

Remove from heat and let cool partially. Add the vanilla. Spread a small amount of custard into the bottom of a 1 1/2-quart casserole. Cover with a layer of vanilla wafers and top with a layer of sliced bananas. Pour about 1/3 of custard over the bananas. Layer the vanilla wafers, bananas and custard to make three layers of each, ending with custard.

Preheat oven to 450 degrees. Beat egg whites until stiff but not dry. Add the sugar and tartar and beat until stiff peaks form. Spoon the meringue on top of the pudding. Spread over the entire surface and seal the edges well. Bake at 425 degrees for 5 minutes.

Yields: 8 servings

Margaret Young

◆ NO-BAKE COOKIES ◆

2	cups sugar
6	tablespoons cocoa
1	teaspoon vanilla
1/2	cup milk
1	stick margarine
2 1/2 to 3	cups rolled oats

On stove top, combine the sugar, cocoa, vanilla, milk and margarine in a medium saucepan and cook over medium heat. Cook to the soft ball stage. Remove the saucepan from the stove and mix in the rolled oats. Drop onto wax paper. Cool completely.

Yields: 48 cookies

Betty Young

◆ BROWNIES ◆

2	1-ounce squares unsweetened chocolate
1	stick margarine
1	cup sugar
2	eggs
3/4	cup all-purpose flour
1/2	teaspoon baking powder
1/2	teaspoon salt
1	teaspoon vanilla
1/2	cup nuts

Preheat oven to 350 degrees. In a medium saucepan, melt the chocolate and margarine. Add the sugar and eggs and stir well. Add the flour, baking powder, salt; mix and add vanilla. Stir in nuts. Pour into an 8-inch square pan. Bake at 350 degrees for 25 to 30 minutes.

Yields: 16 brownies

Eleanor Helms

♦Microwave Brownies♦

Brownie:

2	cups all-purpose flour
2	cups sugar
1	stick margarine or butter
1/2	cup vegetable shortening
1	cup strong brewed coffee or water
1/4	cup dark, unsweetened cocoa
1/2	cup buttermilk
2	eggs
1	teaspoon baking soda
1	teaspoon vanilla

Frosting:

1	stick margarine or butter
2	tablespoons dark cocoa
1/4	cup milk
3 1/2	cups confectioners' sugar, unsifted
1	teaspoon vanilla

To prepare the brownies: In a large mixing bowl, combine the flour and sugar. In a microwave-safe dish, combine the margarine, shortening, coffee or water, and cocoa. Microwave at high power for 2 minutes or until just boiling. Pour the boiling mixture over the flour mixture. Stir to blend. Add the buttermilk, eggs, baking soda, and vanilla. Mix well. Pour batter into a 9x11-inch microwave-safe dish. Microwave at medium high power for 18 minutes, turning the dish every 4 to 5 minutes until brownies test done. They may still appear soft on the surface.

To prepare the frosting: Combine the margarine, cocoa and milk in a microwave-safe dish. Microwave at high power for 2 minutes, stirring once. Add the sugar and vanilla. Stir to blend and frost.

Pat Rush

◆ BLOND BROWNIES ◆

Rich and smooth--a chocolate lover's delight!

2 2/3	cups all-purpose flour
2 1/2	teaspoons baking powder
1/2	teaspoon salt
2/3	cup vegetable shortening
1	box brown sugar
3	eggs
1	12-ounce package semi-sweet chocolate chips

Preheat oven to 350 degrees. Sift together the flour, baking powder and salt and set aside. In a large sauce pan, melt the shortening. Stir in the brown sugar and allow to cool. Beat in the eggs, one at a time. Add the flour mixture and mix. Add the chocolate bits.

Pour into a 15x10-inch, greased and waxed-paper lined pan. Bake at 350 degrees for 25 to 30 minutes.

Yields: 36 to 48 squares

Margaret Young

◆ LEE'S BLOND ◆
BROWNIES

2	sticks butter, melted
1	box dark brown sugar
3	eggs
3	cups all-purpose flour
1	teaspoon vanilla
1	12-ounce package semi-sweet chocolate chips
1	cup chopped pecans

Preheat oven to 350 degrees. Cream the butter and brown sugar. Add the eggs, one at a time. Add the flour, vanilla, chocolate chips and pecans.

Line a 9x13-inch pan with tinfoil. Spread the mixture in the pan and bake at 350 degrees for 20 to 25 minutes. Cut before completely cool.

Yields: 24 to 36 brownies

Eleanor Helms

♦Mini-Chip Blondies♦

3/4   cup margarine or butter, softened
1 1/2   cups packed light brown sugar
2   eggs
2   tablespoons milk
1   teaspoon vanilla
2   cups all-purpose flour, unsifted
1   teaspoon baking powder
1/4   teaspoon baking soda
1/4   teaspoon salt
2   cups (12-ounce package) "mini-chips" semi-sweet chocolate chips

Preheat oven to 350 degrees. Cream the margarine and sugar until light and fluffy. Add the eggs, milk and vanilla. Beat well. Combine the flour, baking powder, baking soda and salt. Add to the creamed mixture. Stir in the chocolate chips. Spread the batter into a greased 13x 9-inch pan.

Bake at 350 degrees for 30 to 35 minutes. Cool completely and cut into bars.

Yields: 36 bars

Deborah Alston

◆ MARSHMALLOW ◆ BROWNIES

1	stick margarine
2	1-ounce squares unsweetened chocolate
3/4	cup all-purpose flour
1/2	teaspoon baking powder
3/4	teaspoon salt
3	eggs
1	cup sugar
1	teaspoon vanilla
1	cup nuts
2	cups sugar
1/2	cup milk
1/4	cup white syrup
1 1/2	1-ounce squares unsweetened chocolate
1	teaspoon vanilla
2	tablespoons margarine or butter
	Marshmallows, cut into halves, or jar of marshmallow cream

Preheat oven to 350 degrees. Melt the margarine and chocolate and set aside. Combine the flour, baking powder, salt. Add the eggs to the flour mixture, mixing well after each addition. Add the melted mixture. Mix well. Add the sugar, vanilla and nuts, and beat well. Pour into a well greased, 13x9-inch pan. Bake at 350 degrees for 25 minutes.

In a medium saucepan, combine the sugar, milk, syrup, chocolate, vanilla and margarine. Bring the mixture to a boil and boil for 2 minutes. Beat until the mixture is the right consistency to spread. Top brownies with marshmallows or marshmallow cream, then spread with frosting.

Yields: 36 brownies

Margaret Young

♦ BUTTERSCOTCH ♦
MARSHMALLOW BROWNIES

1/2   *cup butterscotch morsels*
1/4   *cup margarine or butter*
3/4   *cup all-purpose flour*
1/3   *cup firmly packed brown sugar*
1   *teaspoon baking powder*
1/4   *teaspoon salt*
1   *egg, slightly beaten*
1/2   *teaspoon vanilla extract*
1   *cup semi-sweet chocolate chips*
1   *cup miniature marshmallows*
1/2   *cup chopped pecans or walnuts*

Preheat the oven to 350 degrees. Combine the butterscotch morsels and margarine in small a saucepan and cook over medium heat, stirring occasionally, until the morsels are melted. Remove from heat and set aside.

In medium-size bowl, stir together flour, brown sugar, baking powder and salt. Add the butterscotch mixture, egg and vanilla, mixing well. Stir in the chocolate chips, marshmallows and pecans.

Spread mixture in a greased 9-inch baking pan. Bake at 350 degrees for 20 to 25 minutes.

Cool completely and cut into squares.

Yields: 24 brownies

Margaret Young

◆ CARAMEL BROWNIES ◆

1	German chocolate cake mix
1	stick margarine or butter, softened
2/3	cup evaporated milk
1	12-ounce package chocolate chips
1	cup chopped pecans
1	bag Kraft caramels

Preheat oven to 350 degrees. Combine the cake mix, 1/3 cup evaporated milk and margarine. Pour 1/2 of the mixture into a greased 9x13-inch pan. Press down. Bake at 350 degrees for 6 minutes.

Remove from the oven and sprinkle chocolate chips and nuts on top.

In the microwave, melt the caramels with 1/3 cup evaporated milk. Pour the caramel mixture over chips and nuts. Add remainder of the cake batter over top of caramels. Bake at 350 degrees for 20 to 25 minutes.

Cool completely before cutting. They may not look done, but are.

Yields: 24 brownies

Jackie Brown

♦ EAT MORES ♦

A most requested recipe.

1	stick margarine, melted
1	cup sugar
2	eggs, slightly beaten
1	teaspoon vanilla
3/4	cup all-purpose flour
1/8	teaspoon salt
1/2	teaspoon baking powder
1	cup chopped pecans
1	cup chopped dates

Preheat oven to 350 degrees. Mix the margarine, sugar, eggs and vanilla. Sift the flour, salt and baking powder and mix into the creamed mixture. Add the pecans and dates. Grease a 9-inch pan and line with waxed paper and grease again. Bake at 350 degrees for 30 to 40 minutes.

Yields: 24 bars

Pat Rush

◆ GOODY BARS ◆

1	white cake mix
1	stick margarine melted
1	egg
3/4	cup pecans, chopped
1	8-ounce package cream cheese, softened
1	box confectioners' sugar
2	eggs
1	3-ounce can of coconut

Combine the cake mix, margarine and egg and mix well. Batter will be stiff. Pour the batter in an ungreased 9x13-inch pan. Press the pecans into the dough.

In a medium bowl, combine the cream cheese, sugar and eggs. Using an electric mixer, beat the cream cheese mixture at medium speed. Add the coconut to the cream cheese mixture. Pour the mixture over the top of the dough. Bake at 350 degrees for 40 to 45 minutes.

Yields: 24 bars

Margaret Young

◆ NUT BARS ◆

Bars:

1	stick margarine, melted and cooled
1/2	cup light brown sugar, lightly packed
1	cup all-purpose flour, sifted

Topping:

2	eggs
1/4	teaspoon salt
1	cup light brown sugar
1	teaspoon vanilla
1	tablespoon all-purpose flour
1	cup finely chopped nuts
1	3 1/2-ounce can flaked coconut

To make the bars: Preheat oven to 350 degrees. Mix the margarine and sugar and cream until fluffy. Stir in the flour until blended. Spread into the bottom of a well-greased 13x9-inch baking pan and bake at 350 degrees for 10 minutes.

To prepare the topping: Combine the eggs, salt, sugar, vanilla, and flour. Mix well. Add the nuts and coconut and stir. Pour into the pan and bake at 350 degrees for 20 minutes. Let cool. Sift confectioners' sugar over top

Yields: 24 bars

Margaret Young

◆ BUTTERSCOTCH ◆
PRALINE BARS

2	6-ounce packages butterscotch morsels
1/4	cup margarine
1	cup firmly packed light brown sugar
2	eggs
1/2	teaspoon vanilla
1	cup all-purpose flour, sifted
1	teaspoon baking powder
3/4	teaspoon salt
1/2	cup nuts, chopped

Melt 1 package of butterscotch morsels and margarine. Add the sugar and mix well. Let cool. Add eggs and beat. Add the vanilla and stir. Sift the flour, salt and baking powder together. Add the flour mixture to the sugar mixture, and stir until flour is blended. Stir in the nuts.

Grease a 9x13-inch pan. Spread the mixture evenly. Bake at 350 degrees for 20 to 25 minutes, until it cooks away from side of the pan. Remove from oven. Sprinkle 1 package of butterscotch chips over top. Let the chips melt about 5 minutes and spread the butterscotch evenly over the top of bars. Remove the bars from the pan while warm, but not hot.

Yields: 24 bars

Margaret Young

◆ BROWN SUGAR BARS ◆

2	sticks (1 cup) margarine or butter, melted
4	cups brown sugar
4	eggs
2	cups all-purpose flour
2	teaspoons baking powder
1	teaspoon salt
2	teaspoons vanilla
1	cup pecans, chopped

Preheat oven to 350 degrees. Cream the margarine and brown sugar. Add the eggs, one at a time. Add the dry ingredients and mix. Add vanilla and pecans and stir. Pour into a 9x13-inch greased pan. Bake at 350 degrees for 50 minutes.

Yields: 24 bars

Margaret Young

◆ CHINESE CHEWS ◆

3/4	cup all-purpose flour, sifted
1	cup sugar
1	teaspoon baking powder
1/4	teaspoon salt
1	cup chopped dates
1	cup chopped English walnuts
3	eggs, well beaten

Preheat oven to 300 degrees. Sift the flour, sugar, baking powder, and salt. Stir in the dates, walnuts and eggs. Pour into a greased 10x15-inch pan. Bake at 300 degrees for 30 minutes.

Yields: 36 bars

Margaret Young

◆ MICROWAVE ◆
LEMON SQUARES

1	14-ounce can sweetened condensed milk
1/2	cup lemon juice
1	teaspoon lemon peel, optional
1/3	cup margarine
2	cups graham cracker crumbs
1/3	cup brown sugar

Combine the milk, lemon juice and lemon peel. Mix well and set aside in an 8x8-inch dish. Microwave the margarine on high for 1 minute. Add 1 1/2 cups of graham cracker crumbs and sugar to the margarine, blending well. Reserve 1/2 cup of the crumb mixture to use as topping. Press the remaining crumb mixture firmly in dish. Pour the milk and lemon juice mixture over crumb mixture. Sprinkle the reserved crumbs over top. Microwave on medium-high (70 percent) for 10 to 12 minutes. Cool and cut into squares.

Yield: 16 bars

Margaret Young

♦ LEMON BARS ♦

Crust:
2   *sticks (1 cup) margarine or butter, softened*
2   *cups all-purpose flour, sifted*
1/2   *cup confectioners' sugar, sifted*

Filling:
4   *large eggs, at room temperature*
2   *cups granulated sugar*
      Grated peel of 2 lemons
6   *tablespoons lemon juice*
1   *tablespoon all-purpose flour*
      Pinch salt
1/2   *teaspoon baking powder*
1 1/2 *cup nuts, chopped*

Preheat oven to 325 degrees. Beat the margarine, flour and sugar until fluffy. Bake at 325 degrees for 15 minutes in a 9x13-inch greased pan.

Beat the eggs and sugar until light. Add the peel and lemon juice and mix. Add the flour, salt, baking powder, and nuts and mix. Pour the mixture over the warm crust. Return to the 325 degree oven and bake 35 minutes or until set.

Yields: 24 bars

Margaret Young

◆ GOLDEN BARS ◆

Crust:

1 1/2	cups all-purpose flour
1/2	cup brown sugar
1	stick margarine

Filling:

2	eggs, well beaten
1	cup brown sugar
1 1/4	cups coconut
1/2	cup chopped pecans
2	tablespoons all-purpose flour
1/2	teaspoon baking powder
1/4	teaspoon salt
1/2	teaspoon vanilla

Glaze:

1	tablespoon margarine or butter
2	tablespoons lemon juice
1	cup confectioners' sugar

To prepare the crust: Preheat oven to 275 degrees. Combine the flour, sugar and margarine and mix well. Pour into a 9x13-inch pan. Bake at 275 degrees for 10 minutes.

To prepare the filling: Preheat oven to 350 degrees. Combine the eggs, sugar, coconut, pecans, flour, baking powder, salt and vanilla. Mix well. Pour the mixture over baked crust and bake at 350 degrees for 20 minutes. Remove and glaze with the combination of margarine, lemon juice, and powdered sugar.

Yields: 24 bars

Margaret Young

◆ APPLE SQUARES ◆

1	cup salad oil
2	eggs
2	cups sugar
2 1/2	cups all-purpose flour
1	teaspoon baking soda
1	teaspoon salt
1	teaspoon baking powder
1	teaspoon cinnamon
1	cup pecans
3	cups diced apples, unpeeled
1	16-ounce package butterscotch morsels

Preheat oven to 350 degrees. Mix the oil and eggs. Sift the sugar, flour, baking soda, salt, baking powder and cinnamon together. Add the floured mixture to the creamed mixture and mix well. Add the pecans, apples, and 3/4 of the butterscotch morsels. Spread the mixture into a 9x13-inch greased pan. Put the remaining butterscotch morsels on top of the mixture. Bake at 350 degrees for 55 to 60 minutes.

Yields: 24 bars

Pat Rush

◆ Spicy Apple Bars ◆

1/4   cup margarine
1   cup brown sugar
1   egg, slightly beaten
2   cups chopped apples
1/2   teaspoon vanilla
1   cup all-purpose flour
1/2   teaspoon baking soda
1/4   teaspoon salt
1   teaspoon cinnamon
1/2   teaspoon nutmeg
1/2   cup chopped nuts
   Confectioners' sugar

Microwave the margarine for 30 to 60 seconds. Blend in the brown sugar, egg, apples, vanilla, flour, baking soda, salt, cinnamon, nutmeg and nuts. Mix well.

Grease the bottom of a 10x6-inch microwave-safe dish and spread the mixture evenly in it. Microwave the mixture, uncovered, on high power for 7 1/2 to 8 1/2 minutes, or until no longer doughy rotating dish twice. Cool. Sprinkle with confectioners' sugar.

Yields: 36 bars

Margaret Young

◆ CARAMEL ◆
OATMEAL CHEWIES

1 3/4   *cup oatmeal, uncooked*
1 1/2   *cups all-purpose flour*
3/4   *cup firmed packed brown sugar*
1/2   *teaspoon baking soda*
1/4   *teaspoon salt, optional*
1 1/2   *sticks margarine, melted*
1   *cup chopped peanuts*
1   *cup semi-sweet chocolate chips*
1   *12.5-ounce jar caramel ice cream topping*
1/4   *cup all-purpose flour*

Preheat oven to 350 degrees. Grease a 13x9-inch baking pan. Combine the oats, flour, brown sugar, baking soda, and salt and mix well. Stir in the margarine, mixing well until blended. Reserve 1 cup of mixture. Press the remaining mixture onto the bottom of the baking pan. Bake 10 to 12 minutes or until light brown. Cool 10 minutes.

Top with the nuts and chocolate chips. Mix the caramel topping and 1/4 cup flour until smooth. Drizzle the caramel mixture over the chocolate chips to within 1/4-inch of pan edges. Sprinkle with the reserved oat mixture. Bake an additional 18 to 22 minutes or until golden brown. Cool.

Yields: 32 bars

Pat Rush

◆ FRUIT BARS ◆

1 1/2	cups all-purpose flour, sifted
1	teaspoon cream of tartar
1	teaspoon cinnamon
1/2	teaspoon baking soda
1/2	teaspoon ground cloves
1/4	teaspoon nutmeg
4	eggs
1	cup light brown sugar, firmly packed
1/4	cup raisins
1/4	cup candied cherries, halved
1/4	cup chopped candied citron
1/4	cup chopped walnuts

Preheat oven to 350 degrees. Butter 15x10-inch jelly-roll pan. Sift the flour, cream of tartar, cinnamon, baking soda and ground cloves and nutmeg.

In a large bowl, beat the eggs with an electric mixer until light. Gradually beat in the brown sugar, beating until again light. With wooden spoon blend in flour mixture, then the raisins, cherries, citron and walnuts. Pour into a prepared pan. Bake at 350 degrees for 15 minutes. Cool in pan on wire rack.

Cut into 3x2-inch inch bars. Decorate with confectioners' sugar at serving time.

Yields: 24 bars

Margaret Young

◆ AFTERNOON DELIGHT ◆
DESSERT

1 1/2   *cups all-purpose flour*
1 1/2   *sticks margarine*
1/2   *cup nuts, chopped*
1   *8-ounce package cream cheese, softened*
1   *cup confectioners' sugar*
1   *9-ounce container Cool Whip*
2   *packages instant chocolate pudding*
3   *cups milk*

Preheat oven to 325 degrees. Melt the margarine. Add the flour and nuts and mix. Spread in a greased 9x13-inch pan. Bake at 325 degrees for 15 minutes. Cool completely.

Cream together the cream cheese, sugar and 1 cup Cool Whip. Spread over first layer. Chill 1 hour.

Blend the pudding and milk for 2 minutes. Pour over second layer. Chill 1 hour.

Spread remainder of the Cool Whip. Sprinkle on more nuts and/or chocolate chips. Chill for several hours.

Yields: 6 to 8 servings

Jackie Brown

◆ CHOCOLATE ◆
BUTTERCREAM SQUARES

Crust:

1/4	cup margarine or butter
1/2	cup sugar
1	egg, beaten
1	1-ounce unsweetened chocolate, melted
1/2	cup all-purpose flour
1/4	cup nuts

Filling:

2	tablespoons margarine or butter, softened
1	cup confectioners' sugar
1	tablespoon cream
1/2	teaspoon vanilla

Icing:

1	1-ounce square unsweetened chocolate, melted
1	tablespoon margarine or butter

To prepare the crust: Preheat oven 350 degrees. Grease and flour an 8x8-inch pan. Cream butter and sugar, add egg and chocolate. Then add flour and nuts. Pour into prepared pan and bake at 350 degrees for approximately 10 minutes.

To prepare the filling: Combine the margarine, sugar, cream and vanilla. Blend well and spread on cooled crust.

To prepare the icing: Combine the chocolate and margarine and mix well. Spread on the dessert and chill.

Yields: 24 small bars

Martha Helms

◆ PECAN TARTS ◆

A holiday favorite.

Crust:
1/2	stick margarine or butter
1	small package cream cheese
1	cup all-purpose flour

Filling:
1	egg
3/4	cup brown sugar
1	tablespoon margarine
1	teaspoon vanilla
	Dash salt
3/4	cup pecan pieces

To prepare the crust: Combine the margarine, cream cheese and flour. Chill the dough for 2 hours. Roll into 12, 2-inch balls and place in an ungreased muffin tin. Press the dough along the bottom and sides of each muffin.

To prepare the filling: Preheat the oven to 325 degrees. Combine the egg, sugar, margarine, vanilla, and salt and beat. Pour 1/2 of the pecans into the bottom of the muffins. Pour the mixture into the muffins. Pour the remaining pecans on top of the mixture. Bake for 325 degrees for 25 minutes. Cool well before removing.

Yields: 12 tarts

Margaret Young

◆ FESTIVE FUDGE ◆

2   cups sugar
2/3   cup Pet Evaporated Skimmed Milk
12   regular marshmallows
1/2   cup margarine or butter
        Few grains salt
1   6-ounce package semi-sweet chocolate chips
1   cup chopped nuts
1   teaspoons vanilla

In a heavy 2-quart saucepan, combine the sugar, milk, marsh-mallows, margarine and salt. Cook, stirring constantly, over medium heat to a boil. Boil and stir 5 minutes more. Remove from heat.

Stir in the chocolate chips until completely melted. Stir in the nuts and vanilla. Spread in a buttered 8-inch square pan. Cool.

Yields: 2 pounds

Margaret Young

◆ FUDGE ◆

4	cups sugar
1	12-ounce can evaporated milk
1 1/2	12-ounce packages semi-sweet chocolate chips
1	stick margarine
1	7-ounce jar marshmallow cream
2	cups nuts, black walnuts or pecans

Combine the sugar and milk. Stir and bring to a hard boil for 6 minutes, stirring in the middle but not the sides. Add the chocolate chips, margarine, and marshmallow cream and beat for 3 minutes. Add the nuts and pour the fudge into a 9x13-inch pan.

Yields: 5 pounds

Margaret Young

◆ EASY MINT FUDGE ◆

4	cups sugar
1	12 ounce can evaporated milk
1/2	cups butter or margarine
1	12-ounce package chocolate mints
1/2	pound marshmallows (about 32)
	Nuts

Combine the sugar, milk and margarine. Cook to soft ball stage, 234 degrees to 236 degrees, stirring constantly. Remove from heat. Add the mint wafers and marshmallows. Stir until blended. Add the nuts and pour in buttered pan. Cut into squares when cool.

Yields: 4 pounds

Margaret Young

◆ SOUR CREAM FUDGE ◆

1 1/2   *cups sugar*
2/3   *cup sour cream*
1/2   *cup margarine or butter*
1   *8-ounce white confections coating, finely chopped*
1   *teaspoon vanilla*
3/4   *cup chopped nuts*

Grease an 8-inch pan and set aside. Combine the sugar, sour cream, and margarine in a sauce pan. Cook over medium high heat, stirring with wooden spoon. Use a candy thermometer and stir constantly. Cut heat to a low boil at 238 degrees. Remove and stir in white confection coating and vanilla. Stir until confection is melted. Add nuts stirring until smooth and creamy, about 3 minutes. Pour in pan and cool.

Yields: 2 pounds

Margaret Young

331

◆ Chocolate ◆
Butterscotch Fudge

2	*cups brown sugar*
1	*cup granulated sugar*
1	*cup evaporated milk*
1	*stick margarine or butter*
1	*7-ounce jar marshmallow cream*
1	*teaspoon vanilla*
1	*6-ounce package butterscotch morsels*
1	*6 ounce package chocolate chips*
1	*cup nuts*

Combine the sugars, milk and margarine. Bring the mixture to a boil, stirring constantly. Boil for 10 minutes moderately, stirring occasionally. Remove from heat, add the marshmallow cream and vanilla and stir until smooth.

Add the butterscotch morsels to 2 cups of the mixture and stir. After morsels have melted, add 1/2 cup nuts and stir. Pour into greased 9x11-inch pyrex dish.

Add the chocolate chips to the remainder of the mixture. Stir well until the morsels are melted. Add 1/2 cup nuts. Pour over butterscotch mixture and chill.

Yields: 3 pounds

Eleanor Helms

◆ BUTTERSCOTCH ◆ FUDGE

2 1/4   cups firmly-packed light brown sugar
1   cup granulated sugar
1   stick margarine or butter
1   cup evaporated milk
2   6-ounce packages butterscotch flavored morsels
1   7 1/2 or 10-ounce jar marshmallow cream
1   cup chopped English walnuts
1/2   cup golden raisins (do not use dark raisins)
1   teaspoon rum extract
1/2   teaspoon vanilla extract

In a large saucepan, combine the sugars, butter and milk. Stir over medium heat until butter is melted. Cook about 15 to 18 minutes, stirring occasionally until mixture forms a soft ball when small amount is dropped into cold water or 238 degrees on candy thermometer.

Remove from heat. Stir in butterscotch morsels and marshmallow until thoroughly blended. Add walnuts, raisins, rum and vanilla extracts. Pour into 2 greased 8-inch pans. Cool.

Yields: 3 1/2 pounds

Margaret Young

◆ CARAMEL FUDGE ◆

5   cups sugar, divided
2   cups half-and-half
1/4   cup butter
1/2   cup milk
2   cups miniature marshmallows
1   teaspoon vanilla extract
1   cup chopped pecans

Combine 4 cups sugar, half-and-half, and butter in a heavy Dutch oven. Cook over low heat, stirring gently, until sugar dissolves. Cover and cook over medium heat 2 to 3 minutes.

Sprinkle remaining 1 cup sugar in a large heavy skillet; cook over medium heat, stirring constantly, until sugar melts and turns light golden brown.

Pour caramelized sugar and milk into fudge mixture. (Mixture will lump but will become smooth with further cooking). Cook over low heat, stirring constantly, until caramelized sugar dissolves. Continue cooking, without stirring, until mixture reaches soft ball stage at 240 degrees. Cool to 150 degrees. Add marshmallows and vanilla. Beat with a spoon until marshmallows melt and mixture begins to thicken. Stir in pecans. Pour into a greased 9-inch pan, spreading with a spatula. Cool and cut into squares.

Yields: 5 pounds

Margaret Young

♦ PECAN PRALINES ♦

2	cups unsalted butter
2	cups white sugar
2	cups dark brown sugar
3	tablespoons water
5	cups whipping cream
1	cup ground pecans
3	teaspoons vanilla
2	cups whole pecans

In a 16-inch skillet, melt the butter. Add the sugars and water; cook for 3 minutes, stirring continuously. Add the cream and ground pecans. Bring to a rapid boil and stir continuously for 12 to 18 minutes at 240 degrees on candy thermometer. Add the vanilla and whole pecans. Cook rapidly until 260 degrees on candy thermometer. Using 2 large spoons (one for scraping the other), spoon rounds rapidly onto wax paper. Pralines will cool and harden within 10 minutes.

Yields: 4 pounds

Margaret Young

◆ PECAN BRITTLE ◆

1	cup pecan pieces
1	cup sugar
1/2	cup light corn syrup
1/8	teaspoon salt
1	tablespoon margarine or butter
1	teaspoon vanilla extract
1	teaspoon baking soda

Line a 15x10-inch jelly roll pan with aluminum foil. Butter foil and set aside.

Combine the pecan pieces, sugar, syrup and salt in a heavy 2-quart saucepan. Cook over low heat, stirring gently, until sugar dissolves. Cover and cook over medium heat for 2 to 3 minutes to wash down sugar crystals from the sides of the pan.

Uncover and cook to hard crack stage at 300 degrees. Stir in butter, vanilla and baking soda. Pour mixture onto buttered foil, spreading thinly. Let cool. Break into pieces.

Yields: 1 pound

Margaret Young

♦ MILKY WAY ♦
ICE CREAM

4	Milky Way candy bars
1	large can evaporated milk
1 1/4	cups sugar
6	eggs
1/2	pint whipping cream
	Dash of salt
1	teaspoon vanilla
1/3	cup Hershey's chocolate syrup
	Whole milk to fill freezer

Melt the candy bars in the milk over medium heat, until dissolved. Add the sugar, eggs, whipping cream, salt, vanilla and chocolate syrup and mix well. Pour into a freezer container. Add the milk to fill the freezer container. Churn ice cream.

Yields: 1 gallon

Martha Helms

♦ PEACH ICE CREAM ♦

2	cups mashed peaches
1	cup sugar
1	can sweetened condensed milk
1/2	teaspoon almond extract
3	eggs, beaten
1/2	pint heavy cream
1	quart milk

Combine the peaches, sugar, milk, almond extract, eggs and cream. Mix well. Add the milk and stir. Pour into an freezer container and freeze as directed.

Yields: 1 gallon

Margaret Young

♦ OREO COOKIE ♦ ICE CREAM

3	large egg yolks
1	14-ounce can sweetened condensed milk
2	tablespoons water
4	teaspoons vanilla extract
1	cup coarsely crushed Oreo Cookies
1	pint whipping cream, whipped

In a large bowl, beat the egg yolks; stir in the condensed milk, water and vanilla. Fold in the cookies and whipped cream. Pour into aluminum foil-lined 2-quart container. Cover and freeze for 6 hours or until firm. Scoop the ice cream from pan or peel off foil and slice. Return leftovers to freezer.

Yields: 2 quarts

Margaret Young

◆ OREO COOKIE ◆
ICE CREAM DESSERT

25	Oreo cookies, crushed
1/3	cup margarine, melted
1/2	gallon ice cream (vanilla, coffee, or Baskin-Robbins Jamaican Fudge)
2	tablespoons butter
1	cup powdered sugar
4	1-ounce squares unsweetened chocolate
1	small can evaporated milk

Mix the cookies and margarine and put into greased 9x13-inch pan. Spread the softened ice cream and freeze until hard.

Melt together the butter, sugar, chocolate and evaporated milk. Mix well. Cool and spread on top of the frozen ice cream layer. Freeze until ready to serve.

Yields: 24 servings

Martha Helms

◆ ICE CREAM 'N ◆ CHOCOLATE RICHES

1	box Chocolate Famous Wafers (plain chocolate), crushed
2/3	cup margarine, melted
1/2	gallon ice cream (butter pecan, coffee, or butter almond), softened
5	1-ounce squares unsweetened chocolate, melted
2	tablespoons margarine or butter
1	cup sugar
1	13-ounce can evaporated milk

Combine the crushed wafers and margarine. Spread the crumb mixture on the bottom of 9x13-inch cake pan. Chill.

Spread the softened ice cream on the chocolate crust. Freeze until hardened.

Combine the chocolate, margarine, sugar, and milk. Cook over medium heat, stirring well. Bring to a boil and stir until thickened. Cool slightly. Pour over refrozen ice cream and chocolate crust. Freeze.

Yields: 24 bars

Eleanor Helms

♦ RICH HOT ♦ FUDGE SAUCE

1/2	stick margarine
2	1-ounce squares unsweetened chocolate
1	large can evaporated milk
1 1/4	cups sugar
1 1/2	teaspoons vanilla

Melt the margarine and chocolate. Add the milk and stir. Add the sugar and vanilla. Cook until thick.

Yields: approximately 2 cups

Margaret Young

♦ HOT FUDGE SAUCE ♦

2	1-ounce squares unsweetened chocolate, broken
1	cup sugar
2/3	cup hot milk
1	teaspoon vanilla
	Dash salt

In a blender, add the chocolate, sugar, vanilla, salt. Pulse. Pour the hot milk in slowly through blender hole. Pour sauce into double boiler and heat over boiling water until thickened.

Yields: approximately 2 cups

Margaret Young

◆ CHOCOLATE SAUCE ◆

5   1-ounce squares semi-sweet chocolate
1/2   cup margarine
3   cups confectioners' sugar
1   large can evaporated milk
1 1/4   teaspoon vanilla

Melt the margarine and chocolate. Add the sugar and milk alternately. Cook until thick. Then add vanilla.

Yields: approximately 2 cups

Eleanor Helms

◆BUTTERSCOTCH SAUCE◆

2   tablespoons butter
3/4   cup brown sugar
1/2   cup light corn syrup
1/3   cup heavy or light cream
        Few grains salt

Cook the butter and sugar over low heat until it forms a soft ball in cold water at 234 degrees.

Cook slightly, stir in the cream and add the salt. Serve warm or cold. Sauce will thicken as it cools.

Yields: 1 1/4 cups

Margaret Young

♦ EULOGY ♦

Gladys Biggers Allen

*Granny, who was called "Mee Maw" by her
grandchildren, passed away on
January 19, 1994. The following eulogy was
delivered by her son-in-law, H. Parks Helms.*

As Granny's health deteriorated, we realized that her death was near. My cousin Deborah and I were concerned that the minister who would perform her funeral service would have never known Granny or what her life had meant to us. We agreed to prepare a written summary of her life for the minister so he could mention some of our memories in the service. When Granny passed away, I sat before my computer and let the thoughts and tears flow. Later, Mom called me to let me know that Uncle Parks would be delivering the Eulogy. He was returning from a business trip to Germany and would be home in time for the funeral. I placed my notes in an envelope and left them for Parks, thinking they might be helpful in preparing his speech.

I will never forget sitting on the front row of the church with the family around me, when Parks began the Eulogy. As he spoke, I recognized many of his words. With tears streaming down my cheeks, I leaned over and told my husband, "I wrote that, Sam." Parks later told me it was a blessing to pick up my notes and find many of his own memories in writing. Park's Eulogy is our celebration of Granny's life and all that she has given us.

GLADYS BIGGERS ALLEN
JANUARY 22, 1994

Flying back across the Atlantic Ocean yesterday gave me a great opportunity to reflect on the life and death of Gladys Allen.

In remembering Mee Maw, it is important that we consider not only the way she lived, but the way she died - for in her living and in her dying she has reminded us of the perfect example of Jesus Christ.

Mrs. Allen was an early "women's libber." She ran the family business and raised five children after Paul Allen's death in 1951. At the time of his death, her youngest daughter Eleanor, was 12 years old. Her oldest son Paul, Jr. was at war in Korea.

She had to learn to drive while raising her children and running the family business. We all remember with great joy the time Mee Maw was returning from Clover visiting her sisters with a live rooster in the front seat and buttermilk in the back seat. When the rooster flew to the back seat, she ran off the road and had a wreck (not *too* serious). When they returned to get the car the next day, the rooster was still alive in the back seat - but the buttermilk had spilled and the car had to be sold!

Her living was centered around her family. She welcomed her daughter-in-law and sons-in-law as members of the family. She never criticized them - she only chastised her children when she thought they were not good enough to their spouses. She was always there to help her children. As they started out in their marriages, she loaned them money to get started and let them stay in the downstairs apartment to help make ends meet. She was always there with words of encouragement and helped us all find the good in ourselves.

She was always there for her ten grandchildren. She was there to help her daughters and daughter-in-law following the birth of their children. Quietly, she would clean the house, cook and tend to the baby, while the new mother recuperated.

For the grandchildren, spending the nights with Mee Maw were common occurrences. You always got up early on Sunday to go to Park Road Baptist Church for Sunday School and Church Services. (The family joke was that Mee Maw always showed up early to turn on the heat and lights). On Sunday afternoon, you'd then have fried chicken and rice (sure wish we had that recipe) at the old house on Willow Oak.

Favorite "to dos" at Mee Maw's for the grandchildren included trips to Freedom Park to ride the rides, feed the ducks and go to the Nature Museum. You could always talk Mee Maw into a good movie. Among her favorites were the *Sound of Music* and *Mary Poppins* (and just about any Disney movie).

During those days, you often saw Mee Maw in her 1963 Chevrolet Impala (aqua blue) with a brood of grandchildren in tow. She was always there for her sisters and sisters-in-law, for folks who had worked for her in the family business and for friends from church. And, she loved to go to Clover to stay a week or more with her sisters.

She was always collecting old clothes from family members in grocery sacks. She'd deliver them to folks like Elmiria and Harvey, who had worked for years in the family business. She wanted to make sure that they were all right and would help them with their problems.

She always visited her friends from Sunday School. She spent many a Saturday afternoon visiting her friends in nursing homes.

When she moved to her condominium at the Kimberly, she looked after folks in the building. She passed along food to folks in the building to make sure that they had something good to eat.

A southern lady who truly lived her faith rather than preach it, Gladys' faith was the cornerstone of her life and her family's life. She understood and lived the life described by the Apostle Paul in his letter to the Ephesians: *"For by Grace you have been saved through faith; and this is not your own doing, it is the gift of God, not because of works, lest any man (or woman) should boast. For we are His workmanship, created in Christ Jesus for good works, which God prepared beforehand that we should walk in them."*

Few of us have any memories of Gladys being angry. After five children and ten grandchildren, that's a miracle. Her first priority was to give money to the church and other religious organizations. Her charitable contributions always well exceeded the permitted tax deductions.

Gladys' faith and character became the core of our family. She was the timber which held us together. Her example of love, faith, and character helped us and continues to help us to become better people.

As a family, we learned much from her decline in later life with Alzheimers. We found that there are in fact angels on earth. At the Kimberly, Lou, Lillian and Roberta took care of Mee Maw. They worked with the daughters to help make her life as comfortable as possible.

When physically she required a wheel chair to get around, the family found Wesley Nursing Home. There, she met a wonderful lady named Mrs. Helms, who watched over her and made sure that she had her afternoon chocolate ice cream.

The staff at Wesley cared for Mee Maw with much love and compassion. Many of the aides laughed and sang for Mee Maw just to get a smile. When she was dying, these same angels came in to tell her good-bye. One of the aides, who was home sick with the flu, came in just to see her one last time. She stood there with family members, tears streaming down her cheeks.

There is no way our family can thank these angels enough for what they did for Mee Maw. You've earned your wings, and rest assured that when your day comes, you will join Mee Maw in heaven. Today, as we look back on the life of Gladys Biggers Allen we are thankful that she was a part of our lives. While physically she may no longer be with us, she will always be as close as our hearts for the love and joy she shared with us. She lives on through her sisters and brother, her children, her grandchildren, her great-grandchildren and her friends.

As the plane touched down last night at Dulles International Airport in Washington, it was very clear to me that God has given us a perfect example in the living and dying of Gladys Biggers Allen. She has shown us that a life of loving and giving will be richly rewarded. And even though her death was slow - and some-times painful - we can celebrate today because of the way she lived and the way she died. She has taught us that death has no sting - that the grave has no victory.

We give you praise and thanksgiving, Heavenly Father, for the living and loving and dying of Gladys Biggers Allen.

In Loving Memory of Gladys Biggers Allen
May 16, 1902 - January 19, 1994

Remarks by H. Parks Helms

♦ INDEX ♦

♦ Order Forms ♦

Carolina Publishing Company
Post Office Box 972
Apex, North Carolina 27502

Please send me ___ copies of *Granny's Drawers* at $20.45 per copy ($16.95 plus $3.50 postage and handling). North Carolina residents add $1.02 sales tax. Enclosed is my check or money order for $_____, made payable to Carolina Publishing.

PLEASE PRINT:

Name: _____

Address: _____

City: _____ State: _____ Zip: _____

Allow 2-3 weeks for delivery. For information regarding over-night or international delivery, please call 800-256-9908.

- -

Carolina Publishing Company
Post Office Box 972
Apex, North Carolina 27502

Please send me ___ copies of *Granny's Drawers* at $20.45 per copy ($16.95 plus $3.50 postage and handling). North Carolina residents add $1.02 sales tax. Enclosed is my check or money order for $_____ made out to Carolina Publishing.

PLEASE PRINT:

Name: _____

Address: _____

City: _____ State: _____ Zip: _____

Allow 2-3 weeks for delivery. For information regarding over-night or international delivery, please call 800-256-9908.

◆ ORDER FORMS ◆

I would like to see *Granny's Drawers* in the following stores:

Store Name: _____

Address: _____

City: _____ State: _____ Zip: _____

Store Name: _____

Address: _____

City: _____ State: _____ Zip: _____

- -

I would like to see *Granny's Drawers* in the following stores:

Store Name: _____

Address: _____

City: _____ State: _____ Zip: _____

Store Name: _____

Address: _____

City: _____ State: _____ Zip: _____